TALES OF OLD TOKYO

The Remarkable Story of One of the World's Most Fascinating Cities

John Darwin Van Fleet

"Nowhere else in the world can you see in the streets girls and women in kimonos, either vividly coloured or subdued according to their age, young women in Paris models, girls in jeans, or Indian saris, or neat Chinese dress; mothers leading their children by the hand, or carrying them on their back, or pushing them in prams; men in shorts, in work happi, in the uniform of ten different armies . . ."

From Meeting with Japan *by Fosco Maraini, 1960*

EARNSHAW
BOOKS

Tales of Old Tokyo

By John Darwin Van Fleet

ISBN-13: 978-988-82734-5-4

Copyright © 2015 John Darwin Van Fleet

HISTORY / Asia / Japan

First printing Summer 2015
Second printing November 2015

EB068

Published by Earnshaw Books Ltd. (Hong Kong).

Introduction

Tokyo. Probably the most populous city in the world in the early 19th century. Invasion by foreign navy in 1853. Revolution in 1868. Consumed by fire in 1872. Meteoric return to the top rank of worldwide cities by the end of the 19th century. Capital of the first non-Western country to defeat a Western power in war (1905). Devastation by earthquake and fire, killing more than 100,000 (3% of the total population) in 1923. Descent into fascist nightmare in the 1930s.

Devastation by fire-bombing, again killing more than 100,000, in 1945. Population reduced by half, as the survivors fled. Meteoric rise (again) to the top rank of worldwide cities by the 1960s, as Japan became top five in global GDP. Host of the Olympics in 1964.

Is there any city in human history that has experienced so much shock, so much change, in such a short time? The Japanese famously like to consider themselves exceptional—the history of their

The 'Black Ships'—an image of the U.S. navy's second mission to force open Japan, in 1854.

The old Shinbashi Station, where Tokyo's Shiodome Station now stands, circa 1890

capital city since the mid-19th century gives them abundant reason to conclude that Tokyo is, historically speaking, unique.

Tokyo's sense of exceptionalism, and its instability, are grounded in part in geology. The city rests uneasily on the far eastern edge of the massive Eurasian tectonic plate, which underlies most of Europe and northern Asia, but Tokyo is also within a short bus or boat ride of at least three other tectonic plates: the Okhotsk (north), Pacific (east) and Philippine (south). No wonder then that Japan, host landmass for about 3% of the world's people, also hosts a disproportionate share of the world's most deadly earthquakes.

From 1853 to 1964, Tokyo experienced not only natural cataclysms—the earthquakes and subsequent fires, and policide by firebombing—but also social

transformations hard to fathom in their magnitude: the enforced opening of the capital and the country to foreign trade and residence beginning with Commodore Perry's 1853 invasion, the transformation of the governmental system in the late 19th century and the concurrent modernization at breath-taking

Tokyo street scene, 1947. The banner announces the launch of an annual charitable campaign that continues today.

speed, the subsequent rise of Japan to become one of the world's leading economies and military powers, marked by their (Pyrrhic) victory in the Russo-Japanese War (1904 – 1905), the sociocultural promise of the Taisho Democracy period (roughly 1915 – 1930) destroyed by creeping fascism, the militarization of the capital from that point until 1945, the occupation by the U.S. from August 1945 and yet another total transformation of every aspect of society, and the evolution from the utter devastation of 1945 into one of the world's leading cities, capital of a country that had clawed its way back up to the top five in global GDP, by the time of

the Tokyo Olympics in 1964.

I lived in Tokyo from 11 July 1991 until 20 December 2000, the decade that followed the infamous bubble economy of the 1980s — yet another transformation. I thank Earnshaw Books for the opportunity to construct *Tales of Old Tokyo* as one of EB's *Tales of Old* series.

'Construct' is the correct verb — rather than offering lots of my own prose, in the spirit of the other works in the *Tales of Old* series I have mostly cobbled together the words of those who knew Tokyo first-hand between 1853 and 1964, along with images created during those years.

Note on name order: In the

parts of the body of the work that I've constructed (not including the acknowledgements at the back), I present Japanese people's names in their usual order, family name first, given name second. I present Western names in their usual first name/last name order. Quotations are, to the degree possible, precise in (mis)spellings, etc.

Among the more than three hundred images in *Tales of Old Tokyo*, virtually all are so old that they are now in the public domain. We have attempted at the back to cite some of the more recently published works from which we have sourced images. We regret any omission and will correct it in updated versions of *Tales of Old Tokyo*.

Tokyo's Nihonbashi in the days when one could easily see Mt. Fuji from it, circa 1860

Foreigners flying the Japanese flag at the closing ceremony of the Tokyo Olympics, 24 October 1964

The annual October O-Eshiki festival at Ikegami Honmon-ji, in today's Ota ward of Tokyo, circa 1930

Chronology

8 July 1853	Commodore Perry and his Black Ships arrive in Edo Bay.
31 March 1854	The Convention of Kanagawa, the treaty between Japan and the U.S., signed in Edo, formally ending 250 years of Japan's self-enforced seclusion from the rest of the world.

11 November 1855	Ansei Edo earthquake and fires kill approximately 10,000 Edo residents.

An early 19th century etching of a geisha and her servant

1858	Japan-U.S. Treaty of Amity and Commerce, the 'Harris Treaty', signed.
24 March 1860	Chief Minister Ii Naosuke assassinated just outside the Sakuradamon gate of what was then the Shogun's palace—the Sakuradamon Incident.

Samurai outside a nobleman's house, 1870s

1867 – 1870	Fukuzawa Yukichi publishes the best-selling, multi-volume *Things Western*, establishing himself as the country's leading authority on the West.
4 July 1868	Battle of Ueno marks the end of the Shogunate. The last Shogun, Tokugawa

Mutsuhito, the Meiji emperor, at the beginning of his reign, 1867

Yoshinobu, had resigned months before.

July 17, 1868   Edo renamed Tokyo.

1869   16-year-old Mutsuhito, the Meiji emperor, is moved from Kyoto to the recently renamed city.

A young samurai off to the dojo, the practice hall for martial arts, 1870s

1870   Tokyo's first bakeries and ice cream shops appear.

1872   Massive fire devastates much of downtown; the Ginza and Marunouchi areas are rebuilt using (fireproof) brick, hence gaining them the nickname 'bricktown'. Japan's first railway line opens, linking Tokyo's Shinbashi with Yokohama.

Yukichi Fukuzawa and bride

An early Meiji-era political row

1874   First Western-style restaurants open, in Ueno.

1876   Wearing of samurai swords restricted.

1877   Yamagata Aritomo, one of the 'elder statesmen' (*genro*) of Meiji era, creates a mansion and park named Chinzan-so, now the Four Seasons Tokyo.

A 19th century fishing family, and a large one at that

1878   The Tokyo Stock Exchange and the first chocolate shops open.

1882   Japan's first zoo opens, in Ueno Park.

A peasant with a lovely backdrop

1883	The Rokumeikan, or Deer Cry Pavilion, opens, near the present-day Tokyo Station. Tokyo's first Chinese restaurant, the Kairakuen, opens in Nihonbashi.
1885	Ito Hirobumi appointed as first Prime Minister.
1887	Futabatei Shimei publishes *Drifting Clouds*, Japan's first 'modern' novel.
1888	Japan's first coffee shop opens, in Ueno.
1890	The Ryounkaku, the 'Cloud Surpassing Pavilion', opens in Asakusa. Imperial Rescript on Education signed by the Meiji emperor.
1895	Citywide celebrations for the victorious troops returning from the first Sino-Japanese War. Fried pork cutlets (*tonkatsu*) first offered in a Ginza restaurant – queues form.
22 March 1897	First issue of the *Japan Times*.
11 February 1899	The Meiji Constitution, the country's first written legal foundation, largely written by Ito Hirobumi, announced by the emperor.
1905	Japan wins the Russo-Japanese War decisively

Stamps of the early 20th century

Tokyo newspaper delivery, 1910s

Bathing, 1910s

9

but Pyrrhically. On 5 September, the Hibiya Incendiary Incident erupts in Tokyo's Hibiya Park, a protest against the Treaty of Portsmouth, under which the Japanese were forced to cede wartime gains back to Russia and forego cash reparations.

A vegetable market in the Kanda district, 1910s

30 July 1912

Meiji emperor dies. Yoshihito, taking the dynasty name Taisho, later enthroned. General Nogi Maresuke, with his wife, commits ritual suicide, 'following in their lord's footsteps', several weeks later at the time of the funeral procession. A horrific fire razes the Yoshiwara during the year.

18 December 1914

Tokyo Station opens.

28 September 1918

Hara Takashi becomes country's first commoner to be named Prime Minister.

1920

Tokyo population exceeds three million; Japan becomes one of the original members of the League of Nations.

4 November 1921

Prime Minister Hara assassinated in Tokyo Station.

Tokyo's Mitsukoshi department store opens a new building in the 1920s.

1 September 1923	Great Kanto Earthquake and aftermath claim the lives of about 130,000 Tokyo residents.
25 December 1926	Taisho emperor dies. Hirohito, becoming the Showa emperor, later assumes the throne.
1927	Asakusa and Ueno are connected by Japan's first subway line, the Ginza Line. Shinjuku's Nakamuraya starts selling 'real Indian curry' – queues form again.

Poster soliciting share purchase in Tokyo's Yamanote Express Line in the 1920s. 'Call us on Aoyama 4056!'

1928	Universal male suffrage, radio broadcasting launched.
1931	Tokyo's Haneda Airport opens.
26 February 1936	The 2-26 Incident, an attempted coup, sees militarists occupy the Diet and other government locations in the city. Several government ministers murdered.

National's new electric iron, 1927

3 January 1939	Yokozuna Futabayama's 69-bout winning streak, begun on 7 January 1936, ends with a loss to *maegashira* Akinoumi.
11 February 1940	Yamaguchi Yoshiko, *aka* Ri Koran, performs at the Nichigeki Theatre in

Listening to an early radio broadcast

Yurakucho. A queue forms from the previous night; many can't get in.

8 December 1941 What the Japanese officially call 'The Pacific War' begins with the attack on Pearl Harbor. Foreign embassies in Tokyo are quarantined.

18 April 1942 The Doolittle Raid strikes Tokyo and other cities – 16 U.S. bombers become the first U.S. military forces to attack Japan since the arrival of the Black Ships.

1944 Tokyo government offers 'rice and porridge meals' to an increasingly starving population, available without ration coupons and therefore quite popular.

Women called moga *('modern gals') on a day out in the 1930s*

9 – 10 March 1945 More than 100,000 Tokyoites killed in a single night's firebombing, hundreds of thousands more die in the subsequent several months of firebombing of the major cities of Japan, with the notable and intentional exception of Kyoto. Tokyo's population had already dropped to half that of 1940.

15 August 1945 Hirohito's radio declaration ends the war.

Emperor-backed forces regain control, here in front of Tokyo's Sanno Hotel, following the attempted coup of 26 February 1936.

2 September 1945	Foreign Minister Shigemitsu Mamoru and General Umezu Yoshijiro sign the surrender document aboard the USS Missouri in Tokyo Bay, followed by General Douglas MacArthur and other Allied representatives.

The front of Tokyo's Nichgeki theatre in March 1943

10 April 1946	First female suffrage in a general election.
29 April 1946	The International Military Tribunal for the Far East (IMTFE), commonly known as the Tokyo Trials, begins at the former headquarters of the Imperial Japanese Army in the downtown Ichigaya area.

June 1946	The Shibuya Incident, a turf war in which nearly 2,000 members of rival *yakuza* gangs battled for supremacy, claims the lives of about a dozen.

Sailors crowd on deck to view the signing of the surrender documents, aboard the USS Missouri.

3 May 1947	New constitution ratified, written largely by General MacArthur appointees. Yasui Seiichiro elected first governor of Tokyo by popular vote.

26 January 1948	The Teigin Incident – 12 die after a thief posing as an Allied occupation health authority distributes

An early manga, Shonen Osha *(Young King), debuts in 1947*

13

what he claimed to be anti-dysentery medicine, but was in fact poison, at a branch of the Teikoku Bank (abbreviation: Teigin) in Shiinamachi, near Ikebukuro.

23 December 1948 Following the conclusion of the Tokyo Trials, Tojo Hideki and six others convicted as Class A war criminals are hung at Tokyo's Sugamo Prison.

Women in the female professional baseball league in 1950

1951 Japan-U.S. Security Treaty signed. General MacArthur relieved of command for insubordination and leaves Japan for the last time.

1953 Television broadcasting begins.

Sports broadcasts in the 1950s led to an explosion of TV sales.

1954 Marunouchi subway line opens, linking Ikebukuro and Ochanomizu.

1955 Sony debuts its first transistor radio.

1956 Japan joins the United Nations.

1958 Tokyo Tower, built in part from recycled tanks from the Korean War, opens.

12 October 1960 Yet another assassination by militarists – Japan

Tokyo street scene in the 1960s

Socialist Party head Asanuma Inejiro is run through with a Japanese sword by Yamaguchi Otoya in Hibiya Hall.

1961
Hibiya subway line opens, connecting Minami Senju and Naka-Okachimachi.

1962
The city's population reaches 10 million, making it the world's largest metropolis, a distinction Tokyo maintains today. The iconic Okura Hotel opens.

1964
New Otani Hotel opens, becoming the tallest building in Tokyo.

1 October 1964
Debut of Japan's first bullet train, the *shinkansen*, linking Tokyo and Osaka.

10 October 1964
Tokyo Olympic Games begin.

The city at dusk, 1970

A Universal Theatre of Pleasures and Diversions

From History of Japan *by Engelbert Kaempfer, 1715*

Even what tends to promote luxury, and to gratify all sensual pleasures, may be had here at as easy as anywhere... a universal theatre of pleasures and diversions. Plays are to be seen daily both in public and private houses. Mountebanks, jugglers who can show some artful tricks, and all show people who have either some uncommon or monstrous animal to show... resort either from all parts of the Empire, being sure to get a better penny here than anywhere else.

Early 19th century geisha house

Such a City!

An 18th century traveller

He came once a year to Edo—such was the rule of the shogun—but the court of the shogun's castle was not all that drew him. It was Edo itself: Such a city! Such noise, so much doing, in the sumo rings, at the Kabuki, and, best of all, the pleasures of the Yoshiwara! He looked at the dozen samurai— those who serve. The samurai always amused him: bully-boys, bare-kneed, in heavy leggings and flopping sandals treading the earth grandly, proud of their gay coats, their crab-shaped armor, the two swords pushed with patterned care through the belts around their hips. They had a professional walk, a cock-on-the-dungheap attitude: the way they cut the air with a swagger, peering out from under their big, round hats with warlike grimaces, with mask-like features.

The Key-note of Japan

Fujiyama is the key-note of Japan. When you understand one you understand the other.

In From Sea to Sea *by Rudyard Kipling, 1913*

From Meeting with Japan *by Fosco Maraini, 1960*

It is not difficult to imagine the sense of awe that must have filled the minds of the remote ancestors of the Japanese when they reached these shores and first set eyes on Fuji, then an active volcano. Surely from the first it must have seemed to them a divine thing, a god or the seat of a god.

Hokusai's Great Wave Off Kanagawa, *1830s, the first and most iconic of his famous* Thirty-six Views of Mt. Fuji

The Streets of Edo

From A Diplomat in Japan *by Ernest Satow, 1921*
Streets were laid out with but little thought of the general convenience, and slight provision for the future. The day of wheeled carriages had not dawned upon Japan. It was sufficient if space were left for handcarts, and the most important Japanese commercial town of the future was thus condemned in perpetuity to inconveniences of traffic, the like of which can be best appreciated by those who knew the central parts of business London fifty years ago . . .

Asakusa market, circa 1870

A lion dancer for hire

Commerce on the street

Cutting Down Any Peasant

Okada Shogi writing about a daimyo *and his samurai in the late 18th century*
The samurai of this period of the Tokugawa dictatorship were as dangerous as they looked. There was nothing to prevent their cutting down any peasant or merchant whom they met. This right was theirs to keep them fierce and strong, ready for service to their lord, their *daimyo*.

Fireworks at Ryogoku, *by Utagawa Toyoharu, early 19th century*

A Geisha Bloom

From Geisha Tora no Maki *by Ryutei Tanehiko, 1830*
The great metropolis of Edo is honeycombed with canals and waterways, and wherever they flow, the water laps and washes the city's many *geisha*. In Yanagibashi, the *geisha* bloom in rivalry like primroses in the grass.

The Frog at the Bottom of the Well

A Japanese noble writes to a British diplomat, 1865
Hitherto there had been a great number of stupid men and ignorant persons in our provinces, who still adhered to the foolish old arguments. They were unaware of the daily progress of the Western nations . . . being like the frog at the bottom of the well.

Foreboding

James Lord Bruce, on his departure from Japan in 1858, quoted in The Nineteenth Century *by Joseph H. Longford, 1919. In 1860, Bruce ordered the destruction of the Old Summer Palace (Yuanmingyuan) outside Beijing.*
A land with a perfectly paternal Government; a perfectly filial people; a community entirely self-supporting; peace within and without; no want; no ill will between classes. This is what I find in Japan in the year 1858 after two hundred years' exclusion of foreign trade and foreigners. Twenty years hence what will be the contrast?

19

Anjin-san

William Adams washed ashore in Kyushu in April 1600, one of about 20 survivors of a hundred original crew of his Dutch ship, in turn one of the few to have remained afloat of the five that had left Rotterdam in 1598. Adams became a personal advisor to the new shogun, Tokugawa Ieyasu, and eventually the most influential foreigner in Japan of the era.

The Japanese gave Adams the name Miura Anjin – 'the pilot of Miura' – his grave is near Nagasaki, and his story became famous in James Clavell's novel Shogun *(1975) and the subsequent TV mini-series in 1980 – in these, he was called 'Anjin-san' – 'honorable pilot'.*

Coming before the king, he viewed me well, and seemed to be wonderfully favourable. He made many signs unto me, some of which I understood, and some I did not. In the end, there came one that could speak Portuguese. By him, the king demanded of me of what land I was, and what moved us to come to his land, being so far off. I showed unto him the name of our country, and that our land had long sought out the East Indies, and desired friendship with all kings and potentates in way of merchandise, having in our land diverse commodities, which these lands had not… Thus, from one thing to another, I abode with him till mid-night.

Adams' letter to his wife, describing his meeting with Tokugawa Ieyasu, excerpted from Letters Written by the English Residents of Japan, 1611 - 1623, *N. Murakami and K. Murakawa, eds., 1900*

Probably the Largest City in the World

From Low City, High City *by Edward Seidensticker, 1983*

In the late eighteenth and early nineteenth centuries, Edo was probably the largest city in the world. The population was well over a million, perhaps at times as much as a million and two or three hundred thousand, in a day when the largest European city, London, had not yet reached a million. The merchant and artisan population was stable at a half million. The huge military aristocracy and bureaucracy made up most of the rest. There were also large numbers of priests, Buddhist and Shinto, numbering, with their families, as many as a hundred thousand persons . . .

Influence in the Yoshiwara

From Musui's Story – The Autobiography of a Tokugawa Samurai *by Kokichi Katsu, 1843 (tr. Teruko Craig, 1983)*

"Shall we have some sushi?" I asked. He nodded. "Come on then, I'll take you somewhere interesting." I led him toward the Yoshiwara . . .

I thought I would give him an idea of my power and influence in the Yoshiwara and took him on a complete tour. I strutted and swaggered, and when I'd decided that he had been sufficiently awed, I led him to the brothel Sanosuchiya and asked for the best-looking woman in the house. We were told that with the cherry blossoms in season the rooms were all booked, but when I let them know who was speaking, a room was opened up straightaway. We stayed until morning and parted company at Morinoshita.

A mid 19ᵗʰ century tea shop

Black Ships

On 8 July 1853, after 250 years of enforced seclusion from the outside world, Tokyo witnessed Commodore Matthew Perry of the U.S. Navy lead a fleet of two smoke-belching steamships and two sloops into Uraga Harbor, due south of what is now downtown. Perry's mission was to open trade with Japan on behalf of the United States.

Representatives of Shogun Tokugawa Ieyoshi, pretending to be higher in rank than they actually were, met Perry at anchor and directed him to sail for Dejima, in Nagasaki, where (Perry knew, having studied the matter) he'd be restricted to secondary trade with the Dutch at one of the few ports where the Tokugawa Shogunate had allowed foreign trade and interaction to occur.

"There was a crowd of people there, all stirred up and making guesses about the burning ships on the horizon. Then those ships came nearer and nearer, until the shape of them showed us they were not Japanese ships but foreign ones . . ."

An anonymous shore-side observer in 1853

The feudal era, cannon-less Tokyo Bay fort in about 1850, which later faced Perry – and some soon-to-be astonished locals.

Astonishment

Bayard Taylor, a New York Tribune correspondent travelling with Perry's fleet, in A Visit to India, China, *and* Japan in the Year *1853*
The sight of our two immense steamers — the first that had ever entered Japanese waters — dashing along at the rate of nine knots an hour, must have struck the natives with the utmost astonishment.

Two images of Perry — not hard to guess which was drawn by a foreigner-hating local. The true demon was inside — five years later, Perry was dead, with alcohol-fueled gout as a contributing factor.

Return from Whence You Came!

From Young Americans in Japan *by Edward Greey, 1882*
Twenty-seven years ago an armed fleet "thundered at the gates of Japan," and, in the name of humanity, requested that its harbors should "be opened to the distressed ships of Western nations." I was a member of that expedition, and heard the haughty reply of the official, which was thus interpreted:

"Return from whence you came. No foreigner is permitted to land on our sacred soil!"

How we received this command is a matter of history.

A Prompt Effect

In Americans in Japan *by Robert Tomes, 1857*
[The Japanese] were now told that the Commodore bore a letter to the Emperor from the President of the United States . . . to this they replied that Nagasaki, in the island of Kiusou, was the only place where any such communication could be received . . .
. . . The Commodore sent back an answer declaring that he would not go to Nagasaki; and, moreover, if the authorities did not remove their boats, which were thronging about the ships, he would disperse them by force. This last piece of intelligence produced a very prompt effect . . .

Futility

From A Diplomat in Japan *by Ernest Satow, 1921*
In view of the expected return of the American ships in the following year, forts were constructed to guard the seafront of the capital, and the ex-Prince of Mito was summoned from his retirement to take the lead in preparing to resist the encroachments of foreign powers. . . But when the intrusive foreigners returned in the beginning of the following year, Japan found herself still unprepared to repel them by force. The treaty was therefore signed, interdicting trade, but permitting whalers to obtain supplies in the three harbours of Nagasaki, Hakodate and Shimoda, and promising friendly treatment to shipwrecked sailors.

People People People

From Japan, A Reinterpretation *by Patrick Smith, 1997*
At the Meiji Restoration Japan was a country of roughly 30 million people. . . .
Edo's population at the moment it became Tokyo was less than a million. Then it began to grow: to more than two million at the end of the Meiji period, to almost four million by 1920, year of the first modern census. In August of 1945, half of the city's 7 million inhabitants were either dead or dispersed in the countryside. Then Tokyo began to grow once more: it reached 7 million again by 1952, and 10 million a decade later. In the 1960s an average of more than a hundred families a day left the old villages for Tokyo and the other cities along the Pacific Coast.

24

Perry's party comes ashore in 1854, despite a year of defensive preparation by the Shogunate. Tokyo's Odaiba district, largely reclaimed from Tokyo Bay, was originally the island location of the attempted cannon defense in the 1850s ('daiba' means 'fort' or 'cannon battery').

Perry hosts the Japanese for a dinner on board his flagship, the Powhatan.

Growing Up in Edo
Once I moved...

From A Daughter of the Samurai *by Sugimoto Etsu, 1926*

Throughout the two-hour lesson, he never moved the slightest fraction of an inch except for his hands and lips. And I sat before him on the matting in an equally correct position. Once I moved. It was in the midst of a lesson. For some reason I was restless and swayed my body slightly, allowing my folded knee to slip a trifle from the proper angle. The faintest shade of surprise crossed my instructor's face; then very quietly he closed his book, saying gently but with a stern air, 'Little Miss, it is evident that your mental attitude is not suited for study today. You should retire to your room to meditate.' My little heart was killed with shame. There was nothing I could do. I humbly bowed to the picture of Confucius and then to my teacher, and, backing respectfully from the room, I slowly went to my father to report as I always did, at the close of my lesson.

Geisha training began early.

26

Iya!

From A Japanese Miscellany *by Lafcadio Hearn, 1901*

The last patient of the evening, a boy less than four years old, is received by nurses and surgeons with smiles and gentle flatteries, to which he does not at all respond . . . There are doctors here . . . doctors that hurt people . . . He lets himself be stripped, and bears the examination without wincing; but when told that he must lie down upon a certain low table, under an electric lamp, he utters a very emphatic "*Iya!*" [no!]

So they lay hands upon him two surgeons and two nurses, lift him deftly, bear him to the table with the red cloth. Then he shouts his small cry of war, for he comes of good fighting stock, and, to the general alarm, battles most valiantly, in spite of that broken arm. But lo! A white wet cloth descends upon his eyes and mouth, and he cannot cry, and there is a strange sweet smell in his nostrils, and the voices and the lights have floated very, very far away, and he is sinking, sinking, sinking into wavy darkness. . . . Now the cloth is removed; and the face reappears—all the anger and pain gone out of it. So smile the little gods that watch the sleep of the dead. . . .

The faces of the little stone Buddhas, who dream by roadsides or above the graves, have the soft charm of Japanese infancy. They resemble the faces of children asleep . . .

Samurai

Common people who behave unbecomingly to the samurai or those who do not show respect to their superiors may be cut down on the spot.
Directive of the Tokugawa Shogunate, 17ᵗʰ century

The Happy Dispatch

From The Japanese Sword and its Decoration *by Helen C. Gunsaulus, 1924*
Up to 1876 all samurai or military men were privileged to carry two swords, the *katana* and the *wakizashi*. The first was the weapon with which they fought, settling personal quarrels and clan feuds, or defending their feudal lord, for whose sake each one was proud and ready to die at any moment. The other, the *wakizashi*, was a shorter weapon generally uniform in decoration with the *katana*, for these two were worn together thrust through the belt, and were spoken of as *dai-sho*, meaning "large and small."

The *wakizashi* was always worn indoors. The *katana*, however, was removed on entering a private house and, as proof of trust in one's host, it was laid upon the *katana-kake*, a rack placed near the entrance. The *wakizashi* was especially dear to the samurai, for with it he could follow his feudal chief in death, or, rather than be taken prisoner by the enemy, he could perform the "happy dispatch." If condemned to death, he was privileged to take his own life rather than suffer the disgrace of public execution.

Practice

In The Dark Side *(2001), author Mark Schreiber explains that Yamada Asaemon, described below, was the dynasty name (eight generations) of Tokyo's equivalent of Lord High Executioner.*
When a policeman was not up to the task [beheading the convicted], Yamada would be summoned from his residence in Hirakawa-cho, just west of Edo castle's inner moat, to do the job. But his main source of income was testing and certifying swords, an activity called tameshi-giri. Good swords did not come cheap, and it made sense to certify that the blade was suitably robust. Yamada made sure buyers got what they paid for. To do this, ropes were tied to the wrists and ankles of a headless corpse . . .

A Very Daring Joke

From The Autobiography of Yukichi Fukuzawa, *1899*

When I first called at the residence of my lord Okudaira in Shiodome without those 'things on my waist' [*the long and short samurai swords*], the officials insisted that I was disrespectful to his lordship to enter the estate thus incompletely dressed.

But I had determined upon the abolition of these things and I used to make this sarcastic remark: "It is only the fool who in this enlightened age would carry around the instruments of murder at his side. And he who carries the longer sword is so much the bigger fool. Therefore the sword of the samurai should better be called the "measuring scale of stupidity."

Many of my colleagues shared this idea. One of them, Wada Yoshiro, once carried off a very daring joke. One evening, he with a few friends had gone for a walk without the swords as usual. While they were walking along they came face to face with a group of bullies swaggering along—a considerable number—with their long swords sticking out from their sides as if the road were too narrow to hold them.

Thereupon Wada, deliberately striding along the middle of the road, began to void urine as he came. It was a ticklish situation, whether the ruffians would move apart to the sides of the road or set upon Wada for a fight. . . . His boldness must have got the better of them; the bullies turned aside and passed by without a word. This may seem a very drastic measure, hardly thinkable in these modern times, but it was not so unusual in those times of turmoil.

Two men with 'those things on their waists' in about 1860. On the left is the Shogunate's chief interpreter for Commodore Perry, Moriyama.

The Shogun's battle-ready defenders, circa 1865

Quakes and Catfish Pictures

On 11 November 1855, a 6.9 magnitude earthquake struck Edo. Nearly ten thousand people were killed, many in the fires that followed, as usual for Edo. A shortage of burial containers forced people to leave bodies in the streets.

*Japanese legend of the time held that earthquakes were caused by a giant catfish (*namazu*) wriggling underground. Moreover, earthquakes were seen as a sign of the gods' discontent with the government. After the shogun's humiliating concession to the United States, and the earthquake, *namazu-e*, 'catfish pictures', became highly popular, with the *namazu* shown in a variety of supernatural roles.*

This lantern implores "Watch out for fire!"

Fires devastate the city in 1855.

Population of Tokyo: 1860 – 1970

Year	Population (1,000s)	% change	Comments
1860	approx. 1,100		
1873	595	-50%	Immediately after the 1868 Meiji Restoration, the city depopulated rapidly as feudal lords' retinues returned to their home provinces, . . .
1898	1,440	250%	. . . but the Meiji era's subsequent urbanization and industrialization saw Tokyo's population nearly triple in the following two decades.
1920	3,700	250%	The city's population nearly tripled again in the two decades preceding the Great Kanto Earthquake of 1923.
1930	5,400	50%	Despite the earthquake's having killed 3% of Tokyoites, and many more evacuating temporarily to avoid the starvation and violence in the street, by 1930 the city's population had grown by 50% over the decade.
1940	7,350	35%	Tokyo absorbed adjacent municipalities in the 1930s, but wartime expansion and centralization also contributed to growth of 35% during the decade.
1945	3,490	- 53%	Mass flight from the threatened cities, the devastation of the 1945 fire bombings and utter economic collapse reduced the population by more than 50% in just five years.
1950	6,280	80%	The rapid recovery of Tokyo is reflected in the population, which again exceed six million by 1950.
1960	9,680	55%	The Korean War proved an economic boon for Tokyo, and the city continued its rapid recovery and growth throughout the 1950s.
1970	11,410	6%	By the time of the Olympics, Japan had regained top-five status in GDP by country, and Tokyo had again become the largest metropolitan area in the world.

Source for figures: www.metro.tokyo.jp

The Inaugural U.S. Ambassador

After Perry's initial forcing of Japan to accept foreign contact, the first U.S. ambassador, Townsend Harris, led the United States' further opening of Japan to US-defined trading terms. Similar to demands made by the British on China 15 years previously, after the first Opium War, Harris and the other members of the initial wave of foreigners demanded extra-territoriality (jurisdiction not by Japanese courts but by the foreign for those resident in the foreign-controlled districts), residence in what was then called Edo, and currency/gold/silver exchange considerations. Japan and the USA signed the Treaty of Amity and Commerce in 1858, largely due to Harris's initiative, so the treaty is also widely referred to as the 'Harris Treaty'. The terms of the treaty inflamed large segments of the samurai class and contributed to the overthrow of the Shogunate in 1868. The highest ranking signer of the treaty on the Japanese side, Ii Naosuke, was assassinated just outside the Shogun's castle two years after the signing, in what became known as the Sakuradamon Incident.

Townsend Harris, inaugrial U.S. ambassador to Japan

An Unpromising Reputation . . .

From He Opened the Door of Japan *by Carl Crow, 1939*
The visit of [Commodore] Perry apparently made an equally powerful impression on Harris, for this dramatic enterprise called his attention to his own rather aimless life. He had had an opportunity to achieve a certain local fame as the president of the Board of Education of New York and the founder of the city's first free library, but among many men in New York he was known only as a tippler and a business failure.

. . . Transformed!

From a 28 December 1919 New York Times Magazine article by William Elliot Griffis, author of Townsend Harris: First American Envoy in Japan
When I returned in 1874 from Japan, having lived under both feudal and imperial Governments, I called on Townsend Harris in the old Democratic Clubhouse, at Nineteenth Street and Fifth Avenue. His first question was, "What do the Japanese think of me?"

How highly Japan thinks and has thought of Townsend Harris is being told today in a drama at the Imperial Theatre in Tokyo, which has been crowded nightly since the play had its premiere last November.

From Japanese Expansion and American Policies *by James Francis Abbott, "sometimes instructor of the Imperial Japanese Naval Academy", 1921*
Unsupported by a powerful fleet, living for over a year in fact without communication with his home country, apparently forgotten in Washington . . . in the midst of a semi-anarchy attendant upon the dissolution of the Shogunate and the restoration of the Emperor, Harris nevertheless maintained a steadfastness of purpose, and displayed a tact and ability that deserve the highest praise. Every sort of obstruction was placed in his way by the Japanese, but in the end he won his way through to the conclusion of a treaty, so skillfully drawn that it served as the model for all subsequent treaties entered into by Japan with other foreign nations. Indeed it served as the basis of Japan's foreign relations until 1899. Harris refused to crawl on his hands and knees before the Shogun, and that monarch respected his prejudices in the matter.

The Rejected Concubine

Tojin Okichi was the concubine of Townsend Harris, allegedly rejected by her people as a result, but the legend doesn't align with the facts. Okichi was sent home by Harris, who complained about her skin quality, after a few days. Thus it was not her service to Harris, but his rejection of her, that caused her people to scorn her as well.

Harris in third position, parading toward the treaty signing with the Shogun in 1855, document carried under a U.S. flag by a bearer behind him

Assassination . . .

The Manifesto of the Sakuradamon Con-
spirators, *who assassinated Chief Minister
Ii Naosuke on 24 March 1860, in front of the
Sakuradamon gate of the Edo castle. (Trans-
lation from James Murdoch's* A History of
Japan, *Volume 3, 1926)*

While fully aware of the necessity for
some change in policy since the coming
of the Americans at Uraga, it is entirely
against the interest of the country and a
stain on the national honour to open up
commercial relations with foreigners, to
admit foreigners into the Castle, to con-

A flyer announcing the assassination of Ii Naosuke

clude treaties with them, to abolish the established practice of trampling on
the picture of Christ, to allow foreigners to build places of worship for the evil
religion, and to allow the three Foreign Ministers to reside in the land. Therefore, we have consecrated ourselves to be the instruments of Heaven to punish
this wicked man, and we have taken on ourselves the duty of ending a serious
evil, by killing this atrocious autocrat.

. . . And Other Killings

From Belli Looks at Life and Law in Japan *by Melvin Belli, 1960*
In the grounds of Meguro temple in Tokyo are the three gravestones of Catholic
fathers who were burned to death upon refusing to renounce Christianity. They
bear no inscriptions, but each bears a cross disfigured . . . they died on a cross.

Cherry blossom viewing in the northern Edo suburb of Asuka, with Mt. Fuji visible in the background

Ninja

Sometimes covert agents, sometimes mercenaries, ninja first appeared in the Warring States period (roughly 1450 through the Battle of Sekigahara, 21 October 1600). By the end of the Tokugawa Shogunate (1867), ninja had become myth-encrusted figures – we have little ability today to separate fact from legend.

During the Edo era, confessions were required, so the government used various ways to coerce them.

What The Hell?!

As the Shogunate was collapsing and the country drifted into civil war in 1867, licentious partying broke out all over the country. Ee ja nai ka, literally "it's OK, isn't it?" or loosely "What the Hell?!", became a rallying cry for these celebrations, which featured drinking, singing and dancing under-clothed through the streets, cross-dressing, sex in public, etc.

A popular belief of the time – that amulets would fall from the sky for the ee ja nai ka *revelers*

35

The Beginning of the End

The Edo era and the rule of the Shogunate were coming to a close. But the seeds of the destruction had been planted long before . . .

From Japan: A Short Cultural History *by George Bailey Sansom, 1931*

But on the whole it is true to say that the peasants were heavily oppressed by members of the knightly order, who soon in their turn were exploited by the rising class of merchants. Then, as the *daimyo* and the *samurai* attempted to transfer their burden of debt to the already overladen shoulders of the farmers, the agricultural economy broke down, and was replaced by a mercantile economy which Japan was unable to support without calling on the outside world. Her history for more than two hundred years is summarised in that brief statement.

Bakufu Troops near Mount Fuji in 1867, *painting by Jules Brunet. 'Bakufu' is the Japanese term for the Shogunate. The shogun would step down later that year, and the revolution begin in earnest the next.*

"Honor the Emperor, Expel the Barbarians!"

This phrase, sonno joi *in Japanese, beloved of hotheads who deluded themselves into thinking that Japan could be closed to 'impure foreign influences', was itself one of myriad imports from ancient China.*

From The Autobiography of Yukichi Fukuzawa, *1899*

Here then was the beginning of the national movement, "Honor the Emperor and Expel the Barbarians." It was claimed that the Shogun was not prompt enough in carrying out the desires of the imperial court which had decreed the expulsion of all foreigners without exception. From this, it was argued that the Shogun was disobedient, was disrespecting the great doctrine of the land, and moreover was catering to foreign aggressiveness.

The period from the Bunkyū era [*early 1860s*] to the sixth or seventh year of Meiji—some twelve or thirteen years—was for me the most dangerous. I never ventured out of my house in the evenings during that period.

An Expensive Insurance Policy

From the 28 December 1919 New York Times Magazine by William Elliot Griffis, author of Townsend Harris: First American Envoy in Japan

Sword fights in Yeddo were the order of the day. Even while I lived in Tokio, 1871 – 1874, assassinations, bloody assaults on Ministers of the Government and on foreigners had been, and were, so frequent, that for my life insurance, negotiated in Gotham, I had to pay a heavy premium. We aliens went armed in those days, for all *samurai* wore swords as part of their daily costume, and foreigner-hating patriots were as thick as the native crows.

At the Imperial University the Government kept us within palisades, and had in its pay a band (bettégumi) of expert swordsmen, to accompany and guard each one of us when we went out on the streets of Tokio. Once, when in valorous temerity I had sneaked off alone, in broad daylight, for a ramble in the country, I came within an ace of being sliced up.

Being Anti-Foreigner

From Julian Street, Mysterious Japan, *1921*

"I was a boy of fourteen," said Viscount Shibusawa, "when your Commodore Perry came to Japan. At that time, and for a considerable period afterwards, I was 'anti-foreigner' — that is, I was opposed to the abandonment of our old Japanese isolation, and to the opening of relations with foreign powers. The majority of thoughtful men felt as I did."

Stereotypical images of foreigners – the Brit couple with the ever-present brolly, the American in an ill-fitting suit

Richardson's Murder

From A Diplomat in Japan *by Ernest Mason Satow, 1921*

On the 14th September [1862] a most barbarous murder was committed on a Shanghai merchant named Richardson. He, in company with a Mrs Borradaile of Hongkong, and Woodthorpe C. Clarke and Wm. Marshall both of Yokohama, were riding along the high road between Kanagawa and Kawasaki, when they met with a train of daimio's retainers, who bid them stand aside. They passed on at the edge of the road, until they came in sight of a palanquin, occupied by Shimadzu Saburo, father of the Prince of Satsuma. They were now

An 1860s daimyo's procession

ordered to turn back, and as they were wheeling their horses in obedience, were suddenly set upon by several armed men belonging to the train, who hacked at them with their sharp-edged heavy swords. Richardson fell from his horse in a dying state, and the other two men were so severely wounded that they called out to the lady: "Ride on, we can do nothing for you." She got safely back to Yokohama and gave the alarm. Everybody in the settlement who possessed a pony and a revolver at once armed himself and galloped off towards the scene of slaughter.

. . . His throat had been cut as he was lying there wounded and helpless. The body was covered with sword cuts, any one of which was sufficient to cause death. . . . The Japanese sword is as sharp as a razor, and inflicts fearful gashes. The Japanese had a way of cutting a man to pieces rather than leave any life in him. This had a most powerful effect on the minds of Europeans, who came to look on every two-sworded man as a probable assassin, and if they met one in the street thanked God as soon as they had passed him and found themselves in safety.

Richardson's killers were not tried (and research indicates Richardson was likely a provocateur), but these two samurai are about to die, with foreigners watching, for the killing of two other foreigners in the 1860s.

Blood Atonement

From O-Heart-San, *by Helen Eggleston Haskell, 1908 – a fictionalized version of a real-life attack in Japan in 1891 on Tsesarevich Nicholas Alexandrovich, later to become Nicholas II, Tsar of Russia, and of the attack's aftermath, which resulted in several cases of* seppuku *(men slitting their stomachs) and* jigai *(women slitting the arteries in the neck). Nicholas II's reign was terminated by Russia's 1917 revolution, and in a basement in central Russia in 1918, his life was famously terminated as well, along with that of his family.*

The young Russian was about to reply laughingly, when a gray-haired officer sprang from the crowd, and, drawing a glittering sword knife from his belt, struck fiercely at the head of the imperial guest. Prince Haru recognized the man as a fanatical Shogun, one of the band that objects to the appearance of foreigners in Japan, an uncle of the young man who had frightened Maid Margery at the palace. With a call for help he jumped from his jinrikisha and hurled himself, unarmed, upon the officer.

Then Tsesarevich Nicholas enjoying a rikisha ride in brighter days

[later]

"What is the matter with everybody?" asked Maid Margery, cheerily. "Has all Tokyo gone mad?"

"Oh, I cannot bear it," whispered O-Heart-San. "The emperor and the young prince are grieving and I can do nothing, nothing."

"It seems to me that everybody is doing everything. Look at the stream of people going by, carrying eggs and barley flour and beautiful vases and embroidery and metal work to the young cesarevitch. I'm sure he will feel well repaid for getting a little, tiny wound on the head when he sees the shiploads of presents that your people are carrying to him. And they say that five nobles committed that terrible thing that you call Hari Kari this morning, and that one little girl has committed Jigai?

"They have helped, then, to blot out the stain on our honorable country" said O-Heart-San. "The emperor will be happy when he hears of their loyalty."

Maid Margery was surprised. "He will be most unhappy when he hears of it, I am very sure."

But O- Heart-San shook her head. "They have atoned for the disobedience of one of the emperor's subjects. They have shown their nobility of heart. And you say a young girl committed Jigai. She must be very happy on the River's Farther Shore for she has been brave and loyal. Perhaps if all the young girls in the kingdom could commit Jigai the disgrace that is breaking our hearts might be wiped out."

Preparation for seppuku

Girls studying caligraphy

Battle of Ueno

The forces seeking to re-establish the emperor's (nominal) primacy and the forces seeking to preserve the Shogunate eventually clashed in civil war, the Boshin War, with a climactic battle at Tokyo's Ueno on 4 July 1868 (15 May on the old calendar). The day-long battle resulted in probably 1,000 deaths and as many dwellings lost, along with the decisive victory of the Imperial forces.

The Work of My School Went Right On

From The Autobiography of Yukichi Fukuzawa, *1899*

In May of the first year of Meiji, there occurred the fierce battle of Ueno. A few days before and after this event, all theaters and restaurants and places of amusement were closed, and everything was in such a topsy-turvy condition that the whole city of "Eight Hundred and Eight Streets" seemed in utter desolation. But the work of my school went right on.

On the very day of the battle, I was giving lectures on economics, using an English text book. Ueno was over five miles away, and no matter how hot the fighting grew, there was no danger of stray bullets reaching us. Once in a while, when the noise of the streets grew louder, my pupils would amuse themselves by bringing out a ladder and climbing up on the roof to gaze at the smoke overhanging the attack. I recall that it was a long battle, lasting from about noon until after dark. But with no connection between us and the scene of action, we had no fear at all.

The Battle of Ueno raging

Father on the Wrong Side

From Gensai Murai, His Life and Works, *by Unkichi Kawai, 1904*

When he was five years old, with his mother and grandfather, he left his native place, removing to his father's official residence at Yedo. Shortly after this removal, the war broke out in Yedo, and a battle was fought between the Shogun's party and the revolutionists; it took place at Uyeno. As his father was on the Tokugawa side, and as his *yashiki* was near to the scene of the battle, his abode was surrounded by the revolutionists, and the shells and balls came breaking through into his house. With the rest of his family, the boy was removed to a safe spot. The battle of Uyeno lasted only one day and the men of the Tokugawa side were dispersed, but on the next day a severe engagement took place in another quarter and his uncle died in this battle.

Posing with Yoshihito, the Taisho emperor, some veterans of the Boshin War decades later.

The Last Samurai

Saigo Takamori (1828–1877) led his troops to victory in Tokyo's Battle of Ueno in 1868, but later led the failed Satsuma Rebellion (1877) in which he died. His statue is a popular attraction in Tokyo's Ueno Park. Edward Zwick's 2003 film The Last Samurai, which starred Ken Watanabe and Tom Cruise, is quite loosely based on Saigo's final years.

Saigo's statue in Ueno Park, circa 1915

The statue after the Great Kanto Earthquake of 1923 – people attached notes to the statue to try to locate loved ones.

Quiet Meditation

From In Praise of Shadows *by Tanizaki Jun'ichiro, 1933*

And surely there could be no better place to savor this pleasure than a Japanese toilet where, surrounded by tranquil walls and finely grained wood, one looks out upon blue skies and green leaves.

As I have said there are certain prerequisites: a degree of dimness, absolute cleanliness, and quiet so complete one can hear the hum of a mosquito. I love to listen from such a toilet to the sound of softly falling rain, especially if it is a toilet of the Kanto region, with its long, narrow windows at floor level; there one can listen with such a sense of intimacy to the raindrops falling from the eaves and the trees, seeping into the earth as they wash over the base of a stone lantern and freshen the moss about the stepping stones. And the toilet is the perfect place to listen to the chirping of insects or the song of the birds, to view the moon, or to enjoy any of those poignant moments that mark the change of the seasons. Here, I suspect, is where haiku poets over the ages have come by a great many of their ideas . . .

. . . The Japanese toilet is, I must admit, a bit inconvenient to get to in the middle of the night, set apart from the main building as it is, and in winter there is always a danger that one might catch cold. But as the poet Saito Ryoku has said, "elegance is frigid." Better that the place be as chilly as the out-of-doors; the steamy heat of a Western-style toilet in a hotel is most unpleasant.

Anyone with a taste for traditional architecture must agree that the Japanese toilet is perfection.

Chrysanthemum viewing

The tea ceremony

Bathing in mid 19th century Edo, a lithograph printed in Perry's first official narratives of his visits to Japan, but suppressed in later issues.

Scary Stories

There are some ghost stories in Japan where - when you are sitting in the bathroom in the traditional style of the Japanese toilet - a hand is actually starting to grab you from beneath. It's a very scary story.
Shigeru Miyamoto of Nintendo, inventor of Super Mario, Donkey Kong, etc.

A New Name, a New Era

On 4 November 1868, the move of Mutsuhito, the Meiji emperor, from Kyoto to the recently renamed Tokyo ('eastern capital'), began, taking most of a month. Moving slowly along the ancient Tokaido ('eastern sea way', the primary road in the country, connecting Edo/Tokyo with Nagoya, Kyoto and Osaka), roughly followed by today's Tokaido Line of the shinkansen bullet train, the entourage of hundreds stopped at the 53 way-stations. Along the way, local residents bowed and chanted 'miya-sama' (lordly prince), which chant became a component of the libretto of Gilbert and Sullivan's operetta Mikado. Sterling and Peggy Seagrave, in The Yamato Dynasty (1999), suggest that Mutsuhito spent the journey sipping sake.

Mutsuhito crosses the Kyobashi ('bridge of the capital'), arriving in the city just renamed Tokyo.

Unsettled Times

From Samurai and Silk by Haru Matsukata Reischauer, 1986, writing about Tokyo in the 1870s

Tokyo was in a sorry state. Parts of the city had been damaged by the fighting in 1868, and the population had dropped sharply after many of the *daimyo* and their retainers had left their residences in Edo.

. . . Tokyo was crammed with fierce-looking soldiers from Satsuma, Choshu, and other western domains. Many of them had bayonetted guns and were dressed in newfangled occidental uniforms like those worn by the soldiers who had stomped into the Hoshino house. The streets were crowded with grandees in palanquins, men on horseback, sword-bearing samurai, peddlers hawking their wares with lacquer boxes on their backs or baskets slung on poles, and artisans and merchants, dressed in their distinctive blue costumes decorated with the trademark or name of their companies and often carrying huge packages on their backs. Because of the unsettled times, there were many beggars in filthy rags, huddled under bridges or in dark corners.

The palace, disheveled, in 1870

Tokyo or 東京 or とうきょう or トーキョー – What's the Difference?

The Japanese language employs four distinct writing systems (from left to right, above): 1) the Roman alphabet used throughout the West and called *romaji* ('Roman characters'), 2) the Chinese characters, called *kanji* in Japan, which Japan imported from China starting around 500 CE and which are a combination of phonetic symbols and logograms, and two phonetic syllabaries, the 3) *hiragana* and 4) *katakana*. *Hiragana* and *katakana* were derived from the *kanji* in the later part of the first millennium CE. Typically the *kanji* are used for centers of meaning (nouns and the roots of adjectives, verbs and adverbs, plus proper names), the *hiragana* are used for linguistic housekeeping (declension of verbs and adverb/adjective modifiers, the Japanese version of prepositions, etc.), *katakana* for representation of *gairaigo* (imported words – 外来語, literally 'language that came in from outside') and the *romaji* as accessories/decoration in a number of ways, plus public signage. One can make the case that this confluence, or perhaps train wreck, of writing systems makes Japanese the most complicated written language in the world.

Sticks, Not Swords

In the second and third years of Meiji, the demand for foreign goods remarkably increased. Those who formerly looked upon them with contempt changed their minds and even dressed in foreign clothes. Our males adopted the European style. They put on fine tall hats instead of wearing large queues [topknots] on their heads, and took to carrying sticks after discarding their swords. They dressed in coats of the English fashion and trousers of the American. They would only eat from tables and nothing would satisfy them but French cookery.
The Tokio Times, 1877

Changing Tastes

From Aguranabe (Sitting Around the Stewpot) *by Kanagaki Robun, 1871*
A man about thirty-five, rather swarthy it is true, but of clear complexion, thanks apparently to the daily use of soap, which purges all impurities. His hair, not having been cut for some hundred days, is long and flowing, and looks as if it is in the process of being let out altogether, in the foreign style. Naturally enough, he uses that scent called Eau de Cologne to give a sheen to his hair. He wears a padded silken kimono beneath which a calico undergarment is visible. By his side is his Western-style umbrella, covered in gingham.

From time to time he removes from his sleeve with a painfully contrived

A meat shop and restaurant in the 1860s

Hair styling and shogi, *the chess of Japan*

gesture a cheap watch, and consults the time. As a matter of fact this is merely so much display to impress others, and the chain is only gold-plate. He turns to his neighbor, who is also eating beef, and speaks:

"Excuse me, but beef is certainly a most delicious thing, isn't it? Once you get accustomed to its taste, you can never go back to deer or wild boar again. I wonder why we in Japan haven't eaten such a clean thing before? For over 1620—or is it 1630—years people in the West have been eating huge quantities of beef. Before then, I understand, beef and mutton were considered the king's exclusive property, and none ever entered the mouth of a commoner, unless he happened to be something on the order of a daimyo's chief retainer. We really should be grateful that even people like ourselves can now eat beef, thanks to the fact that Japan is steadily becoming a truly civilized country. Of course, there are some unenlightened boors who cling to their barbaric superstitions and say that eating meat defiles you so much that you can't pray any more before Buddha and the gods. Such nonsense shows they simply don't understand natural philosophy. Savages like that should be made to read Fukuzawa's article on eating beef."

Making the New Year's greetings rounds, 1860s

Ginza, 2.0

A complete transformation of the Ginza from its role in the Edo era as a silver mint (hence the name – 'Ginza' means 'silver seat') began with a fire that destroyed much of the entire downtown area in 1872. The government rebuilt the area using then-novel brick (fireproof), which led the locals to nickname it 'bricktown'. The country's earliest gaslights were installed at this time.

Ginza in 1872

Ten years later, the streets were paved and railed for horse-drawn trollies. By 1903, horse-drawn trollies were being pushed out by electric-powered ones.

From Madame Sadayakko *by Leslie Downer, 2003, about a young man strolling in the 1880s*

He strolled down magnificent Ginza Street, the pride of the city, where all the buildings were of red brick or stone with glass windows and curtains, just like in the West. He even boarded one of the horse-drawn trams that clattered along metal tracks, driven by natty young men in waistcoats, trousers, and caps. He observed carriages and rickshaws rattling up and down, women in bustles and bonnets, and men in trousers and overcoats. He took it all in, but he was far too phlegmatic to get worked up about it. Even when the Ginza's much-hailed eighty-five electric streetlights – Japan's first experiment with the latest new invention, electricity – flickered on in the evening, he was not mightily impressed.

By the early 1930s, Ginza had this prospect . . .

From Japan as We Saw It *by M. Bickersteth, 1893*

We returned home by the Ginza, the great central thoroughfare of the city. It has footpaths, and many of the shops are very large, and crowded with beautiful specimens of Japanese art. The attempts at English on the signboards in the Ginza and other streets of Tokyo are very amusing. "Wine, beer and other medicines"; "A shop, the kind of umbrella, parasol or stick"; "The shop for the furniture of the several countries"; "Prices, no increase or diminish"; "All kinds of superior sundries kept here"; "Skin maker and seller" (portmanteau shop); "Ladies furnished in the upstair." These are a few specimens; and I always knew we were getting near to S. Andrew's House when we passed "Washins and ironins carefully done."

. . . and by the 1960s, looked like this.

51

The Great Reformer

Fukuzawa Yukichi (1834 – 1901) played an enormously powerful role in the development of Meiji-era Japan. He was a member of Japan's first diplomatic mission to the United States (1859 – 60) and founded a school that eventually became Tokyo's Keio University. His ten-volume Things Western *established him as a leader in Japan's drive to understand and catch up with the West, while the 17-volume* On Learning *bolstered his position as the Meiji era's leading educational reformer.*

"In this school roughness and disregard of others, toward older persons or among fellow students, are prohibited. It is, however, a useless practice for students to bow to teachers and their seniors in the hallways or other busy places in the school precincts. A nod will be sufficient. It is not in accord with the morals of the scholar to waste time in useless etiquette. This announcement is made for the benefit of every member of the school."

Notice posted at Fukuzawa's school, circa 1870

Fukuzawa has been featured on the ¥10,000 banknote since 1984.

Fukuzawa on his morning walk, late 19th century

A Daily Walk

From The Wild Geese *by Mori Ogai, 1913*

Okada had regular routes for his daily walks. He would go down the lonely slope called Muenzaka and travel north along Shinobazu Pond. Then he would stroll up the hill in Ueno Park. Next he went down to Hirokoji and, turning into Naka-cho—narrow, crowded, full of activity—he would go through the compound of Yushima Shrine and set out for the Kamijo after passing the gloomy Karatachi Temple. . . .

There was another route. He occasionally entered the university campus by the exit used by the patients of the hospital attached to the medical school because the Iron Gate was closed early. Going through the Red Gate, he would proceed along Hongo-dori until he came to a shop where people were standing and watching the antics of some men pounding millet. Then he would continue his walk by turning into the compound of Kanda Shrine.

A city of magnificent distances without magnificence.
Isabella Bird, Unbeaten Tracks in Japan, *1882*

Playing at Ueno's Shinobazu Pond, about 1928

The Kudanshita district of Tokyo in 1893

Mori Ogai and family, circa 1900

Royalty from Both Sides of the Ocean

From Japanese Literature, Manners and Customs in the Meiji-Taisho Era *by Kimura Ki, 1957*

President Grant and Mrs. Grant came to visit Japan following his term as president of the United States (1869-1877). At that time there was a Western custom of a man offering his arm to escort a lady into dinner. The person of the Empress, like the Emperor's, was not supposed to be touched. A court official was ready with a dagger to kill President Grant if he touched the Empress. Fortunately, for all concerned, he did not.

U.S. Grant viewing Kegon Falls during his visit in 1879

A Badly Formed Mouth

From A.B. Mitford's account of his meeting Mutsuhito, the Meiji emperor, in 1868

His complexion was white, perhaps artificially so rendered, his mouth badly formed, what a doctor would call prognathous, but the general contour was good. His eyebrows were shaven off, and painted in an inch higher up. His costume consisted of a long black loose cape hanging backwards, a white upper garment or mantle and voluminous purple trousers.

Mitford goes on to mention that the emperor's cheeks were rouged, his lips painted red and gold and his teeth blackened.

Potential Wardrobe Malfunction

A Japanese literary scholar talking to Julian Street, in Mysterious Japan, *1920*

At first, when the Emperor received ambassadors, he wore his ancient imperial robes and was seated upon cushions, Japanese fashion. But the ambassadors were arrayed in brilliant uniforms covered with decorations, and in accordance with their home customs they *stood* in the imperial presence. They would stand before a European king or an American president. Therefore it seemed respectful to them to stand before our Emperor.

But according to our customs, that is the worst thing that can happen. We must always be lower than the Emperor; we must not even look from a second-story window when he drives by.

Can you imagine an Occidental admiral or general, with his tight uniform, heavy braid, and sword, approaching any one upon his hands and knees? It would be foreign to his nature and training, not to say ruinous to his costume.

White Teeth for Women – A Recent Development

In 1873, the Japanese empress consort, Haruko, appeared in public in Tokyo without blackened teeth, creating an uproar. At the time, married women commonly blackened their teeth in Japan and other parts of East Asia, as did, rarely, men, as we see from Mitford's account (facing page). The practice had a practical benefit: retarding dental decay.

Mutsuhito seated with his family circa 1880. Haruko, the empress consort, married Mutsuhito in 1869. She bore none of his fifteen children, but adopted Yoshihito (later the Taisho emperor), here front and center, from one of the dozen or so concubines.

Highly popular imagery of a Japanese wrestler throwing a foreigner

How Many Kids?

Mutsuhito, on a visit to Finance Minister Matsukata's Tokyo home, upon seeing about a dozen children here and there: "How many children do you have?" Finance Minister Matsukata: "Please give me a day to look into the matter."

100 Different Items in One Shop

One of a thousand imported innovations, Japan's first department stores (the Japanese term hyakkaten, *which preceded the more currently common* depaato, *means 'a shop with 100 items') appeared in Ginza in the late 19th century.*

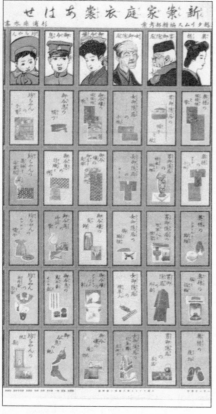

Mitsukoshi's home department store, in Tokyo's Nihonbashi, in the late 1920s. Elevator girls had become high status among Japan's working women by that time.

A turn-of-the-century card game published by one of Tokyo's department store pioneers, Mitsukoshi – no surprise that the items on the cards are products offered by the store.

Another department store in the same neighborhood, the Shiroki-ya, meets an unfortunate fate in December 1932.

Two Island Kingdoms

From Japanese Expansion and American Policies *by James Francis Abbott, 'sometimes instructor of the Imperial Japanese Naval Academy', 1921*
The Japanese like to compare themselves with the English, and their Island Empire to the United Kingdom. Such a comparison has a certain justification. Both are relatively small island groups closely adjacent to a rich and populous continent. Each must depend on a strong navy for national protection. Each is densely populated.

The Wildest Confusion

From Ukigumo *(Drifting Clouds) by Futabatei Shimei, 1877*
Dangozaka was in a state of the wildest confusion. Flower-sellers stood by the usual signboards waving the flags of their respective establishments in the attempt to lure in customers, and the cries of the barkers at every shop entrance got mingled quite unintelligibly in the autumn wind. In the midst of the turmoil all one could see were the feverishly shouting faces of the barkers, who were in the same frantic state no matter how often one looked at them. Not surprisingly, when one went inside the shops the confusion was exactly the same as outdoors.

A Tokyo farewell party for Futabatei Shimei (seated front row, third from right), author of Japan's first modern novel, Drifting Clouds, *in 1908 – he was leaving for Moscow to serve as the Asahi Shinbun's correspondent there, and would die at age 45 on the return journey the next year – tuberculosis – about the same age as George Orwell was when the latter was also felled by tuberculosis in 1950. Futabatei Shimei, a pen name, is a play on what his father said when told of Futabatei's plan to become a writer: kutabatte shimae, roughly 'go to hell!'*

Yazaki Shinshiro commenting on his friend Futabatei Shimei's imperative in writing, 1880s
. . . There were many dialects within Japan and the language varied greatly from place to place, but the spirit, indeed the heart, of Japan was Tokyo, and therefore he had to select Tokyo speech. But he felt that by that time the language of Tokyo had already been corrupted by the many people who came to the capital from other parts of the country. He decided he would have to cull the essence of the language of the Edo period and work from Edo speech.

Raw Fish on Rice

Sushi, Japan's most famous cuisine, was, like so much else Japan is famous for, not originally developed in Japan. But in the mid 19th century, the first recognizably modern version of the cuisine appeared, called edomae-sushi, *with general credit going to Hanaya Yohei (1799 - 1858).*

Why was it named edomae? *Because* edomae *means 'in front of Edo (bay)' – since freshness was a pressing challenge in the era before cold storage and transport, the best place to get fresh fish for sushi was in the nearby bay, and calling a restaurant* edomae *served as a signal of freshness.*

Sushi and other shops along the shore of Edo Bay, circa 1860

Poor but Happy

From Unbeaten Tracks in Japan *by Isabella Bird, 1889*

My impression is that, according to our notions, the Japanese wife is happier in the poorer than in the richer classes. She works hard, but it is rather as the partner than the drudge of her husband. Nor, in the same class, are the unmarried girls secluded, but, within certain limits, they possess complete freedom.

The World's Largest Fish Market

Tokyo's Tsukiji was originally home to the city's first wave of foreign residents, who enjoyed extra-territoriality on the land reclaimed from Tokyo Bay ('Tsukiji' means 'reclaimed land'). Rikkyo University (now in Ikebukuro) and the American School in Japan (now in Tokyo's western suburb of Chofu) trace their roots here. Of the institutions established at that time, only St. Luke's Hospital remains in the area, and Tsukiji has become what this title proclaims, though not for long – the city government is preparing, despite substantial opposition, to move it a few kilometers east, freeing up high-value real estate and creating more opportunities for 2020 Olympic development.

Tsukiji market in 1911

Do You Eat Those Things?

From Young Americans in Japan *by Edward Greey, 1882*

Among the curiosities of the market were party-colored fish, brilliant in red, blue and gold tints, sold alive in glass and porcelain jars. These beautiful creatures capture flies by spouting water over them. The boys also saw any quantity of tiger-marked sea-porcupines and zebra-sols, both of which are eaten by the natives.

While they were watching the scene, the marketmen continued to arrive with enormous fishes, which were dumped upon mats, placed on the ground, and cut up with long, strong knives.

After minutely inspecting the fresh-fish department, the lads visited the side streets, devoted to the sale of the dried sorts—among these being oysters,

Tuna on their way to sushi plates

shrunk out of all shape, mussels, sardines, clams, shrimps, cod, whale and shark.

On the outskirts of the market were many shops and open stalls, devoted to the preparation and sale of cuttle-fish.

The boys halted before a stand where a man was frying the delicacy and chatting to a coolie, who was waiting for a load. The vendor seeing Oto, said, "honorable sir, do you wish to buy some tender slices? I have purchased a cuttle weighing a hundred pounds, and can furnish you with any part of the fish, either fresh or cooked."

"Do you eat those things?" asked Fitz.

"Eat them!" cried the man, "why, they are much sought after and are most delicate in flavor."

Tokyo roadside shop for sushi, in the early 1930s

Connections

Japan's first train line was completed in 1872, connecting Tokyo and Yokohama. Soon lines were running all over the place. When Tokyo's first station, Shinbashi (where Shiodome is now) opened, "those invited to attend the opening ceremony, with its bunting, flags, cannonades and other unfamiliar Western-style trappings, were warned not to turn up in traditional working clothes, hanten jackets or country-style momohiki pants, or to display any form of nakedness." (From Tokyo–A Cultural History *by Stephen Mansfield, 2009). Within ten years, the first legs of what would become the Yamanote loop line were opened, connecting Akabane and Shinagawa and bringing Shinjuku and Shibuya stations to life.*

A geisha, circa 1900, using one of those new-fangled talking machines

The main Tokyo switchboard, circa 1920

The first telegraph lines were installed at about the same time, also connecting Tokyo and Yokohama, shortly followed by telephones.

Is It Really a City?

From Around the World with General Grant *by John Russell Young, 1879*
It is hard to realize that Tokio is a city—one of the greatest cities of the world. It looks like a series of villages, with bits of green and open spaces and inclosed grounds breaking up the continuity of the town. There is no special character to Tokio, no one trait to seize upon and remember, except that the aspect is that of repose.

Why Nippon/Nihon vs. Japan?

'Nippon' and 'Nihon' are Romanizations of 日本, the proper name of the country in Japanese script. So why did the West, and consequently the rest of the world, adopt the name 'Japan'?

Because the West first learned about Japan via ancient China, where 日本 was pronounced something like *zheppen*. Marco Polo spelled the feudal islands' name Cipangu.

One meaning of 日本 is 'where the sun comes from', also in part a Chinese derivation – viewed from east China, the sun seems to rise from the vicinity of the Japanese archipelago. But 'origin in the sun' also reflects the Japanese foundation myth, that the royal family trace their lineage to the sun goddess, Amaterasu.

The Last Beheading – of a Woman

In early Meiji, one O-den Takahashi, working as a prostitute, murdered one of her customers. On 31 January 1879, having been sentenced, she was escorted to the execution grounds at Tokyo's Ichigaya prison. She approached her fate with bravado, but dissolved into wailing as the swordsman approached. His first swing failed to behead her, as did his second, by which time she was a bloody mess. He finally severed her head from her body.

Her genetalia were cut off and put in formaldehyde. They were on display at a department store in Akasaka as late as 1950.

O-den's last moments

At Work in the Meiji Era

Conscription for military service began in the 1870s, and contributed to the defeat of the Satsuma Rebellion (which the Japanese call the Southwestern War) in 1877.

Kabuki performers

Household industry

Carpenters

Shopping Takes Time...

From Japan as We Saw It *by M. Bickersteth, 1893*

... but it must be confessed that Japanese shopping is a decidedly lengthy business. First, a pipe is offered you; then tea; then the least attractive goods are produced; and at last, after much bowing on both sides, the very thing you have desired from the first; but even then it will not be yours until it has been bargained down to a reasonable price. The crape merchant was well accustomed to foreigners, and begged leave to draw up an English bill for my father. It was a delightful production, made out for so much "yellow crepe" (though we had chosen pale blue and mauve), and directed to "Pickastes, Esq."

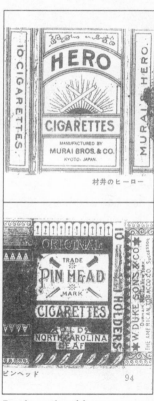

A Tokyo tobacco shop circa 1880

Popular smokes of the era

A Dancing Cabinet

Designed by famed architect Josiah Condor, "the father of modern Japanese architecture," and built near the current site of the Imperial Hotel, the Rokumeikan, or Deer

Cry Pavilion, was aimed at helping leading members of Japanese society interact with the recently-arrived Western intruders, as equals in a Western environment rather than as subjects, which in turn might hasten the end of the unequal treaties. Japan's government at the time earned the pejorative 'dancing cabinet' as a result of their frequenting the Pavilion and practicing their Western dance steps. The Westerners were not as impressed as the Japanese had hoped . . .

Japanese dignitaries, attempting to adopt Western dress and dance steps

> She had a fearsome bonnet of velvet and glass beads which would persist in tumbling backwards, though sternly tied under the chin, and a wrinkled European gown. . . . When she got up a spasm of pain crossed her face at the torture of high-heeled narrow shoes. . . . Her gloves, poor dear, were at least three sizes too large.
>
> *Lewis Wingfield commenting on the Empress at a ball in the 1880s*

A Scratch Formation

From I Am a Cat *by Natsume Soseki, 1905*

I understand that, now for some time, Japan has been at war with Russia. Being a Japanese cat, I naturally side with Japan. I have even been cherishing a vague ambition to organize some kind of Cats Brigade which, if only a scratch formation, could still inflict claw-damage on the Russian horde.

The Cloud-Surpassing Pavilion

*Japan's first skyscraper, the 12-storey Ryounkaku, or 'cloud surpassing pavilion',
built in Asakusa in 1890, also featured the country's first elevator.*

Kubota Mantaro (1889 – 1963), translation from Low City, High City *by Edward Seidensticker, 1983*

In days of old, a queer object known as the Twelve Storeys reared itself over Asakusa.

From wherever you looked, there it was, that huge, clumsy pile of red bricks. From the roof of every house, from the laundry platform, from the narrowest second-floor window, there it was, waiting for you. From anywhere in the vastness of Tokyo, the embankment across the river at Mukojima, the observations rise at Ueno, the long flight of stone steps up Atago Hill, there it was, waiting for you, whenever you wanted it.

Soldiers at the old Aoyama military ground preparing to depart for the first Sino-Japanese war, 1894, and . . .

. . . victory arches erected in Hibiya Park to welcome home the surviving soldiers, 1895

67

Geisha

From a 1920s booklet by Akiyama Aisaburo, quoted in Yoshiwara *by Stephen and Ethel Longstreet, 1970*

The term geisha literally means "accomplished person," and a geisha is needless to say the fair sex, generally very young and good looking, latently playing an important role in the social function of modern Japan. Most geishas are conversant with singing and dancing or with some other light accomplishments, and they wait upon guests as professional entertainers during a dinner or a garden party or the like, to say nothing of certain delicate services occasionally rendered, but of course very furtively.

Now, looking over records in the days of yore, the origin of geisha might be traced indirectly to those women who had been leading a Bohemian life in the Nara period [710-794 A.D.], wandering along coastwise towns in order to offer pleasant hours to provincial dignitaries and travelers on governmental missions. It is said that, being far away from the capital where very little comfort could be had, these officials felt lonely and cheerless, but found a mighty consolation in these women, who had evidently a slight knowledge of poetry and were trained to sing and to dance as well.

From Working Women of Japan *by Sidney Gulick, 1915*

The lives of these girls are pitiful in the extreme. Chosen from among the families of the poor on the basis of their prospective good looks and ability to learn, they leave their homes at an early age and are subjected to the severe drill already outlined. They go through their lessons with rigid, mechanical accuracy. In public they appear in gorgeous robes, their faces painted and powdered, artificially dominating everything about them, clothing, manners, and smiles. As a rule nothing is done to develop their minds, and of course the cultivation of personal character is not even thought of. They are instructed in flippant conversation and pungent retort, that they may converse interestingly with the men, for whose entertainment they are alone designed.

Eminently Distressing to European Ears

From Isabella Bird, Unbeaten Tracks in Japan, *1888, on geisha singing style. The Japanese thought similarly of Western arias and such, and often said so.*

The vocal performance was most excruciating. It seems to consist of a hyena-like howl, long and high, a high voice being equivalent to a good voice, varied by frequent guttural half suppressed sounds, a bleat, or more respectfully an impure shake . . . eminently distressing to European ears.

Rivals

From Japanese Girls and Women *by Alice Bacon, 1899*
Without true education or morals, but trained thoroughly in all the arts and accomplishments that please – witty, quick at repartee, pretty, and always well dressed – the geisha has proved a formidable rival for the demure quiet maiden of good family, who can only give her husband an unsullied name, silent obedience, and faithful service all her life. The problem of the geisha and her fascination is a deep one in Japan.

A geisha at 'home' in about 1920

A Geisha, A Singer, A Founder of the New Government

Tokyoites in the 1890s enjoyed a captivating melodrama involving Sadayakko, one of the country's most famous geisha; Kawakami Otojiro, one of the country's most popular entertainers; and Ito Hirobumi, the country's first prime minister, author of the country's first constitution and the Meiji emperor's closest drinking buddy. Ito had earlier paid a huge sum to be the first to have sex with Sadayakko (a privilege called mizuage, *famously illuminated in Arthur Golden's 1997* Memoirs of a Geisha, *when she was about 15, and then kept her as one of his mistresses. Later, after Ito released her, she married Kawakami, who had by then become a huge star nationwide due in large part to his massively popular satirical song Oppekepe. The geisha and the actor led Japan's first theatrical tour of Europe and the United States, from 1899.*

Kawakami with his signature rising-sun fan

From The Chuo Shinbun, *early 1890s, translation in* Madame Sadayakko *by Leslie Downer, 2004*
"Boss Kawakami staged a real-life love scene with Miss Yakko of the Hamada House at the end of last year. He thought she might become very popular if only she put that cool, stylish beauty of

Ito Hirobumi in the 1890s, 15 years before he was assassinated by a Korean nationalist. His final words were, 'the fool,' because Ito was among the more reasoned Japanese leaders (low base line) in his attitude toward Korean colonization.

Sadayakko and Kawakami (right) after their return from the Western tour, at home in Chigasaki, just south of Tokyo, circa 1905

hers onstage. For her part, she thought he was different from the big-spending, flashy kind of *danna* she usually hangs around with. He was a real man, greatly different from other men who were dumb and weak, like jellyfish or women. Apart from which, no one has ever created such a funny song as 'Oppekepé' in the whole of Japan. So she called him to her side and would not let go. Kawakami, as befits a hero, couldn't leave her either. Or perhaps two or three of his bones had melted, disabling him from acting."

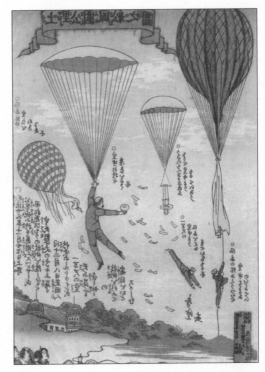

RIGHT: With his balloon antics and parachute jumps, Spencer the Balloon Man also captured the fancy of Tokyo-ites in the 1890s.

Matriculating Women

From A Japanese Interior, by Alice Mabel Bacon, 1894, on the development of the Peeress' School for young ladies, which was eventually occupied by the authorities to house the Peers School for young men, including the future emperor.

I do not think I have written you that a beautiful new brick building has been in process of construction for some time past, to be occupied, as soon as finished, by our school. It is quite near here, and I have watched its growth all winter with great interest, as we thought how pleasant and comfortable the new building would seem after the ramshackle old one that we now occupy. It is all finished now, and workmen are engaged in laying out the grounds, and in taking up the trees and shrubs from our present school-yard to plant them in the new place; for here in Japan, when you move, you carry with you not only your furniture, but your garden as well, shade trees, turf, and all. For months the school authorities have been busy choosing carpets, curtains, and furniture, and the plan was, after the examinations were over, for us to move into the new building for our graduating exercises. We were to have a fine time, and the Empress was to make us a speech in person. Such were our hopes and expectations, but at present they seem likely to suffer an untimely blight.

Women at a university exercise period in the Mejiro district of Tokyo, circa 1910

Bad Habits Be Gone!

From Stories of My Life *by Hani Motoko (1873 – 1957). She was Japan's first female reporter and in 1902 founded* Fujin no Tomo *(Woman's Friend), still published today. She is buried in Tokyo's Zoshigaya cemetery in Minami Ikebukuro, along with Akutagawa Ryunosuke, Lafcaido Hearn, Nagai Kafu, Natsume Soseki and, a bit out of company, Tojo Hideki.*

About one hundred students lived in the dormitory of Meiji Women's School. At seven in the evening, we would gather in the auditorium for a prayer service and stay on to study until nine o'clock. . . .

For a country girl like myself, it was not easy at first to get up early in the morning, to wash in a crowded washroom, and to eat and bathe expeditiously. I took up the challenge and reaped an unexpected dividend: stubborn headaches I had suffered throughout my First Women's Higher School days from constant, indiscriminate reading late into the night stopped. I was cured, moreover, of the bad habit of snacking ingrained as a child growing up in the countryside, where constant nibbling was a way of life . . .

One of the dormitory supervisors, a Mrs. Kuroyanagi, was a widow who combined the graciousness of her native Kyoto with the high spirit worthy of a Tokyoite. Her competent management and creative imagination contributed immensely to our health and enjoyment.

LEFT: *Tsuda Umeko, one of Japan's first female foreign exchange students, who lived in Washington DC from age six to age 18, returning in 1882. She founded in 1900 what would eventually become Tokyo's Tsuda College.*

ABOVE: *A reunion of students from the Peeress' School, circa 1917*

Ueno, Circa 1890

Turn-of-the-20th-century street in front of Ueno Park

From Ukigumo *(Drifting Clouds) by Futabatei Shimei, 1889*

Autumn in Ueno Park. Ancient pine trees stood row upon row, their branches interlaced, their needles thick and luxuriant, of a green so deep as to saturate the heart of an onlooker. The fruit trees were desolate in contrast; old and young alike covered with withered leaves. The lonely camellia bushes, their branches laden with flowers, seemed to yearn for companionship. Several of the delicate maple trees had turned a blazing red. The cries of the few remaining birds mirrored the sadness of the season. All at once, the wind blew sharply.

The branches of the cherry trees shivered and trembled, shaking free their dead leaves. Fallen leaves strewn on the ground rose as if moved by a spirit and danced about in happy pursuit of one another. Then as if by unanimous accord they lay down again. This bleak and dreary autumn scene cannot compare with a bright and hopeful spring day, but still it had a special magic of its own.

Merry visitors on their way to Dangozaka walked among the trees. The tinkling laughter of young girls echoed in the quiet air.

The Center of Japan

From Young Americans in Japan *by Edward Greey, 1882*

The travelers, after going a long distance through narrow streets and over many canals, were trundled over the famed Nippon Bashi (great bridge of Japan) from which they caught a passing glimpse of Fuji-yama.

The bridge, a wooden structure much inferior to many others in the city, was thronged with people, and the noise of their clogs, the rumblings of the carts and other vehicles, and shouts of the *jin-riki-sha* men were almost deafening.

Coolies, carrying enormous fish suspended from bamboo poles, were running to and fro; the bridge being in the vicinity of the largest market in the city, and the landing place for fishermen, who arrived with their finny prizes at all hours of the day.

The boys had been told that all distances in Japan were measured from the Nippon Bashi, so Fitz shouted to Oto,

"Say, where is the first milestone?"

"A mile from here, in any direction," was the laughing answer.

In April 1863, the penultimate shogun, Tokugawa Iemochi, crossed the Nihonbashi on the way to Kyoto, answering a summons by the emperor and becoming the first shogun to visit the imperial capital in more than two centuries. His procession numbered more than 3,000. Seventeen years old at the time, Iemochi had three more years to live.

From The Cities of Japan, *by Harvey Shepard, 1912*
The local government units are not sharply defined. For instance, the Tokyo district, called Tokyo-fu, consists not only of the city and its suburbs, but also of twenty-two towns and one hundred and fifty-six villages contiguous to the city, and of hundreds of small islands, one of which is a thousand miles distant.

Nihonbashi in 1915, four years after the original wood had been replaced by stone

Nihonbashi's 400-year-old famed view of Mt. Fuji was destroyed by the construction of the city's expressways, preparing for the 1964 Olympics, but would have been lost in any event within a few years, because of smog.

Temple of the Goddess of Mercy

The Asakusa Kannon temple, or Sensoji, is Tokyo's oldest temple, dating from the seventh century.

Raree-shows and Penny Gaffs

From A Handbook for Travellers in Japan *by Basil Hall Chamberlain and W.B. Mason, 1891*
The grounds of Asakusa are the quaintest and liveliest place in Tokyo. Here are raree-shows, penny gaffs, performing monkeys, cheap photographers, street artists, jugglers, wrestlers, theatrical and other figures (ningyo) in painted wood and clay, vendors of toys and lollypops of every sort, and, circulating amidst all these cheap attractions, a seething crowd of busy holiday-makers.

Grown-up Men and a Childish Sport

From Unbeaten Tracks in Japan *by Isabella Bird, 1888*
A broad-paved avenue, only open to foot passengers, leads from this street to the grand entrance, a colossal two-storied double-roofed mon, or gate, painted a rich dull red. On either side of this avenue are lines of booths—which make a brilliant and lavish display of their contents—toy-shops, shops for smoking apparatus, and shops for the sale of ornamental hair-pins predominating. Nearer the gate are booths for the sale of rosaries for prayer, sleeve and bosom

The Hozomon entrance to the main temple, which Bird refers to, circa 1920

idols of brass and wood in small shrines, amulet bags, representations of the jolly-looking Daikoku, the god of wealth, the most popular of the household gods of Japan, shrines, memorial tablets, cheap ex votos, sacred bells, candlesticks, and incense-burners, and all the endless and various articles connected with Buddhist devotion, public and private. Every day is a festival-day at Asakusa; the temple

is dedicated to the most popular of the great divinities; it is the most popular of religious resorts; and whether he be Buddhist, Shintoist, or Christian, no stranger comes to the capital without making a visit to its crowded courts or a purchase at its tempting booths.

The temple grounds are a most extraordinary sight. No English fair in the palmiest days of fairs ever presented such an array of attractions. Behind the temple are archery galleries in numbers, where girls, hardly so modest-looking as usual, smile and smirk, and bring straw-coloured tea in dainty cups, and tasteless sweetmeats on lacquer trays, and smoke their tiny pipes, and offer you bows of slender bamboo strips, two feet long, with rests for the arrows, and tiny cherry-wood arrows, bone-tipped, and feathered red, blue, and white, and smilingly, but quite unobtrusively, ask you to try your skill or luck at a target hanging in front of a square drum, flanked by red cushions. A click, a boom, or a hardly audible "thud," indicate the result. Nearly all the archers were grown-up men, and many of them spend hours at a time in this childish sport.

Bird probably wasn't aware that archery was a front for prostitution at the temple, explaining why 'grown-up men' would 'spend hours at a time in this childish sport'.

Acrobats and others on a temple street, circa 1860

The 47 Ronin

From Tales of Old Japan *by A.B. Mitford, 1871*
In the midst of a nest of venerable trees in Takanawa, a suburb of Yedo, is hidden Sengakuji, or the Spring-hill Temple, renowned throughout the length and breadth of the land for its cemetery, which contains the graves of the Forty-seven Ronins, famous in Japanese history, heroes of Japanese drama, . . .

A pre-Meiji exile ship departs with its load of criminals, mourning loved ones left behind.

Winding Up a Priest

From Young Americans in Japan *by Edward Greey, 1882*
After an exceedingly warm walk, the sun being well overhead, the visitors arrived at the temple. They did not linger in the courtyard of the main building, but entered a structure on the left, where they beheld an image of the thousand-armed Kuwannon, and some beautifully executed, life-like carvings, representing Oishi Kuranosuke (Sir Big-rock) and his forty-six loyal comrades.

"How wonderfully natural!" exclaimed the Professor. "One would almost think they were endowed with life."

"How exquisitely they are colored!" said Mrs. Jewett.

"I remember them all," said Sallie. "There is Sir Big-rock, and his brave son, Sir Unconquerable, who was so fond of fighting; Sir Red-fence, who loved his bottle, but loved his honor better. What are you doing, Fitz?"

The boy, who was squinting and peeping behind the figures, turned to a *bozu* who guarded them, and said in a confidential tone, "How do you wind these up?"

"Wind-up!" ejaculated the *bozu* "I – I do not understand your question."

The Professor frowned, and Mrs. Jewett signaled; however, Fitz did not appear to notice them, and continued, –

The samurai of their time — these soldiers, by this time largely conscripted, are being quartered in houses around Tokyo in 1904, the beginning of the Russo-Japanese War.

"Can't you put keys into their backs or sides, and wind up their clock-work?"

"These are figures of great heroes," said the *bozu*. They are not ningiyo (puppets)."

The visitors ascended a pathway leading from the temple to the cemetery which contained the tombs of the forty-seven Ronins.

"This is the place where they washed the head of Sir Kira. See, that inscription says so, and warns people not to lave their hands or feet here," said Sally.

"Why did they bather his head?" demanded Fitz. "Was he sick, or how?"

"He was dead," solemnly answered Oto.

"Oh!" muttered Fitz, "I guess they thought he had only fainted, and hoped to bring him to."

"You must drink some of the water," urged gentle Mrs. Nambo. "They say, those who partake of the well of Sengakuji will be inspired with *Yamato Damashi* (the spirit of old Japan)."

All but Fitz complied with her request.

"I don't want to taste it," he growled. "I'm bad enough without having the *Yamato Damashi*."

The graves at Sengakuji, circa 1910

Fireworks on the Sumida

From My Japanese Prince *by Archibald Clavering Gunter, 1904*

We were being poled down a rather narrow canal which had formerly been one of the old moats of the city; in places its sluggish waters were full of pink lotus flowers. Passing rather five minutes after, we enter the river itself. Upon its waters are a jam of boats, at times so crowded together that an active man can pass from one bank of the Sumida, here some three hundred yards wide, to the other dry shod, jumping from barge to barge.

. . . we all grow hungry and indulge in a picnic repast washed down by iced champagne. As we finish, and the gentlemen light their cigars, night descends, the river becomes a swaying sea of lanterns, not only upon its own liquid surface, but both its banks, some of the tea-houses perched high for view and breeze being literally covered with gorgeous hued things whose many bright colors seem to make this soft summer night a kind of Venetian fete.

Upon a big barge next to us is a band playing, not only Japanese music, but every ragtime tune invented in the United States.

Then high up over the lanterns are more bursting rockets, some of them exceedingly fine, breaking into great bunches of various colored flaming ribbons that seem to float about in the air, and weeping willows of molten gold with red flowers.

A bill from a teahouse, circa 1920, showing JPY26.30 for food, sake and such, and JPY27.80 for 'six sake servers, tips to geisha and their attendants'. JPY50 in the early 1920s was roughly a month's salary for a junior government employee.

Pleasant meals are in progress on nearly all the barges, some quite elaborate, some served European style, others in the Japanese manner. Music is omnipresent, from the big brass band to the sharp voiced samisens and kotos, the Japanese banjo and harp; even in a small row-boat a bronze figure is beating a drum. Since darkness has come upon us, the whole river, banks and waterway, seems a glow of light from myriads of lanterns, some of the overhanging tea houses being covered with thousands of paper moons.

Cleaning up

A less-crowded day on the Sumida River, circa 1930, . . .

. . . and a relaxed fireworks viewing from across the river

A Startling Sight

From Japan Day By Day *by E.S. Morse, 1917*

It was a startling sight when we got near the place to see that the fireworks were being discharged from a large boat by a dozen naked men, firing off Roman candles and set pieces of a complex nature. It was a sight never to be forgotten: the men's bodies glistening in the light with the showers of sparks dropping like rain upon them . . .

Human Horses

From Unbeaten Tracks in Japan *by Isabella Bird, 1888*

The kuruma, or jin-ri-ki-sha, consists of a light perambulator body, an adjustable hood of oiled paper, a velvet or cloth lining and cushion, a well for parcels under the seat, two high slim wheels, and a pair of shafts connected by a bar at the ends. The body is usually lacquered and decorated according to its owner's taste. Some show little except polished brass, others are altogether inlaid with shells known as Venus's ear, and others are gaudily painted with contorted dragons, or groups of peonies, hydrangeas, chrysanthemums, and mythical personages. They cost from 2 pounds upwards. The shafts rest on the ground at a steep incline as you get in—it must require much practice to enable one to mount with ease or dignity—the runner lifts them up, gets into them, gives the body a good tilt backwards, and goes off at a smart trot. They are drawn by one, two, or three men, according to the speed desired by the occupants. When rain comes on, the man puts up the hood, and ties you and it closely up in a covering of oiled paper, in which you are invisible. At night, whether running or standing still, they carry prettily-painted circular paper lanterns 18 inches long. It is most comical to see stout, florid, solid- looking merchants, missionaries, male and female, fashionably- dressed ladies, armed with card cases, Chinese compradores, and Japanese peasant men and women flying along Main Street, which is like the decent respectable High Street of a dozen forgotten country towns in England, in happy unconsciousness of the ludicrousness of their appearance; racing, chasing, crossing each other, their lean, polite, pleasant runners in their great hats shaped like inverted bowls, their incomprehensible blue tights, and their short blue over-shirts with badges or characters in white upon them, tearing along, their yellow faces streaming with perspiration, laughing, shouting, and avoiding collisions by a mere shave.

TOP LEFT: *An eager rikisha puller attempts to persuade a not-so-interested mother, circa 1930, when the advent of the automobile was hastening the end of the rikisha era.*

TOP RIGHT: *A famous painting from 1908 empathetically portraying an impoverished rikisha puller's wife and children*

BOTTOM LEFT: *A satirical magazine of the early 1870s. The horse ('ba') and the deer ('ka') pictures at the top, as a pair, inply 'baka', Japanese for 'stupid'.*

"Not to have written a book about Japan is fast becoming a title of distinction."
Basil Hall Chamberlain, 1890

The Nightless City

The Yoshiwara was Japan's most famous licensed prostitution district, established by the Shogunate in 1617. Prostitution was outlawed by the Japanese government in the late 1950s, but soon thereafter erotic bathhouses exploited loopholes in the law. The district, near the Asakusa Kannon Temple, continues its traditional business today, with the tacit approval of the police.

From Japan: A Short Cultural History *by George Bailey Sansom, 1931*
After the great fires of 1657-1658 the Yoshiwara was removed to a different district, where the bath girls and others assembled. By Genroku *[late 1680s]* it was exceedingly flourishing, and is said to have contained some two thousand courtesans. Known as Fuyajo, or the Nightless City, it was almost self-contained, since it harboured as well as those ladies a numerous population of their attendants, of dancing and singing girls, jesters and other entertainers, together with a most varied collection of tradespeople to supply their needs. Hither resorted not only the young townsmen, but also samurai in disguise, and even high officers of the Shogun or his vassals, while rich merchants were known to give costly fantastic entertainments within its walls. There thus grew up a distinct town, with its own customs, its own standards of behavior, and even its own language.

From Growing Up *by Higuchi Ichiyo, 1895, a reflection on autumn in the Yoshiwara*
Mosquito incense in the shops gives way to charcoal for pocket warmers, the mortars have a sad ring to them, and in the quarter the clock on the Kadoebi seems to have turned melancholy too. Fires glow at Nippori whatever the season, but it is now that one begins to notice them: "That is the smoke from the dead?" A samisen refrain drops down on the road behind the teahouses, and one looks up and listens. It is from the white hand of a geisha. The refrain itself is nothing – "Here, where we pass our night of love" – and yet it strikes the ear with a special poignancy. Guests who make their first visits to the quarter at this time of the year, a woman who used to be there says, are not the lighthearted roisterers of the summer. They are men with a deep seriousness about them.

In those days, nearby Nippori hosted the city's main crematorium. Higuchi probably wound up there herself the next year, when she died of tuberculosis at age 24. Hers is the face on the modern ¥5,000 note.

Police settling a dispute in the Yoshiwara – a daily occurance

Errands during the day, before the customers arrive

From Working Women of Japan *by Sidney Gulick, 1915*

In 1912, a fire completely destroyed the section of the city known as 'Yoshiwara,' which for 300 years has been assigned to prostitution. This center of the social evil had become enormously wealthy, and such magnificent buildings had been erected for the business that it had become one of the famous sights of Tokyo. Before the fire was fairly over, the anti-brothel forces began to organize their campaign, which continued for months. A magazine called Purity (Kaku Sei) was started. In this case, however, success did not crown their efforts.

The 1912 Yoshiwara fire

Men Writing Of Women

The Utmost Modesty

From Bushido, the Soul of Japan by *Nitobe Inazo, 1904*
Girls, when they reached womanhood, were presented with dirks (kai-ken, pocket poniards), which might be directed to the bosom of their assailants, or, if advisable, to their own. The latter was very often the case: and yet I will not judge them severely. Even the Christian conscience with its horror of self-immolation, will not be harsh with them, seeing Pelagia and Domnina, two suicides, were canonized for their purity and piety. When a Japanese Virginia saw her chastity menaced, she did not wait for her father's dagger. Her own weapon lay always in her bosom. It was a disgrace to her not to know the proper way in which she had to perpetrate self-destruction. For example, little as she was taught in anatomy, she must know the exact spot to cut in her throat: she must know how to tie her lower limbs together with a belt so that, whatever the agonies of death might be, her corpse be found in utmost modesty with the limbs properly composed. Is not a caution like this worthy of the Christian Perpetua or the Vestal Cornelia?

Almost No Flesh

From In Praise of Shadows by *Tanizaki Jun'ichiro, 1933*
But when I think back to my own youth in the old downtown section of Tokyo, and I see my mother at work on her sewing in the dim light from the garden, I think I can imagine a little what the old Japanese woman was like. In those days—it was around 1890—the Tokyo townsman still lived in a dusky house, and my mother, my aunts, my relatives, most women of their age, still blackened their teeth. I do not remember what they wore for everyday, but when they went out it was often in a gray kimono with a small, modest pattern.

My mother was remarkably slight, under five feet I should say, and I do not think that she was unusual for her time. I can put the matter strongly: women in those days had almost no flesh. I remember my mother's face and hands, I can clearly remember her feet, but I can remember nothing about her body. She reminds me of the statue of Kannon in the Chuguji.

Envy

In Ukigumo *by Futabatei Shimei, 1889*

"I really wish you could have seen the way the young lady was dressed today. She had on a yellow-striped silk kimono underneath and a gorgeous striped crepe over it. Her hair was coiled around in a bun, the way she usually wears it, but she had on that hairpin she got at the Izumo shop the other day that looks like a rose." She outlined the shape with her hands. "She really and truly was beautiful. What I wouldn't give to have one sash-clip like that." The girl fell silent, brooding about something for a moment.

At the loom in 1910

A Bayside City

It would seem that we Japanese are wholly lacking in the ability to build a city.
Nagai Kafu (1879 – 1959), quoted in Tokyo *by Donald Richie, 1999*

Tokyo, viewed from a plane above what is now Edogawa Ward, circa 1911

Disappointing Interior

From Japan as We Saw It *by M. Bickersteth, 1893*

The Russo-Greek Cathedral, a basilica with walls six feet thick in order to resist earthquakes, is the finest foreign building in Tokyo, and has a great central dome like our own S. Paul's Cathedral. The interior is rather disappointing, empty and whitewashed, except the east end, which is a blaze of gilding and colour, with some fine pictures of saints introduced into it. We climbed up to the roof, and obtained our first uninterrupted view of Tokyo. Very striking it looked, with its dull grey sea of houses, broken now and then by a daimyo's palace and garden, or the roof of a temple, and with the beautiful Bay of Tokyo lying beyond.

What Bickersteth called The Russo-Greek Cathedral is now commonly called the Nicolai Cathedral. It still stands – near Ochanomizu Station.

Dozens of planes flying over the Cathedral in the mid-1930s, as part of air raid defense practice.

Not Inferior to Any

From Handbook of Information for Shippers and Passengers, *by the Nippon Yusen Kaisha, 1904*

With regard to charges, the westward voyage from Yokohama to London or Antwerp cost 500 yen (or about £50) and the eastward voyage from London or Antwerp to Yokohama £55, which figures are considerably cheaper than those charged on other prominent lines, whereas the fare and accommodation on board the Nippon Yusen Kaisha's vessels are not inferior to any. Moreover, liberal rebates are made to Japanese military and naval officers, to diplomats and their families and to missionaries and their families. The western journey from Japan to London occupies 61 days, 10 ports being called at en route – namely, Kobe, Moji, Shanghai, Hong Kong, Singapore, Penang, Colombo, Suez, Port Said and Marseilles.

The long-gone Manseibashi Station, which stood between today's Kanda and Akihabara Stations, circa 1915

Theatre of Outcasts and Riverside Prostitutes

From a speech by kabuki superstar Ichikawa Danjūro IX, 1872

The [kabuki] theatre of recent years has drunk up filth and smelled of the coarse and the mean. It has disregarded the beautiful principle of rewarding good and chastising evil. It has fallen into mannerisms and distortions, it has been flowing steadily downhill. . . I have resolved to clean away the decay.

What Ian Buruma has more recently described as "this theatre of outcasts and riverside prostitutes" (in Behind the Mask, 1984), *transitioned toward not only the respectable, but a 'traditional' dramatic form, beloved of militarists and such, by the 1930s.*

Gorgeous Costumes of Old Japan

From My Japanese Prince *by Archibald Clavering Gunter, 1904*

I soon forgot everything but the extraordinary sensations that came to me at the Kabukiza. Though the Tokyo theatres are usually closed in mid-summer, this was an extra performance, given probably on account of the number of visitors that the lotus festival had attracted to the Japanese capital. At all events, hot as it was, the theatre was crowded.

. . . The two big balconies and the whole pit are occupied by an unusually brilliant audience drawn by a great performance; for the most celebrated actor of his day, Kikiguro, the worthy successor to the late Ichikawa Danjuro, the Salvini of Japan, is in the bill.

Of this wonderful artist's performance, which moved me both to tears and to laughter, his facial expression being so remarkable that I could follow accurately his emotions during each scene, I have little to say; likewise of the curious revolving stage, graceful scenery and brilliant lighting as well as the accurately gorgeous costumes of Old Japan displayed in the only place that they can now be viewed, the national theatre.

An onnagata, *a man playing female roles in kabuki, getting into character, circa 1930*

The Danger of Boy Favorites

From In Praise of Shadows *by Tani-*
zaki Jun'ichiro, 1933
But the Kabuki is ultimately a
world of sham, having little to do
with beauty in the natural state. It
is inconceivable that the beautiful
women of old — to say nothing of
the men — bore any resemblance to
those we see on the Kabuki stage
. . .

. . . the Noh actor, unlike the
Kabuki performer, wears no white
powder. Whenever I attend the
Noh I am impressed by the fact that
on no other occasion is the beauty
of the Japanese complexion set off
to such advantage — the brown-
ish skin with a flush of red that
is so uniquely Japanese, the face
like old ivory tinged with yellow.
A robe woven or embroidered in
patterns of gold or silver sets it off
beautifully, as does a cloak of deep
green or persimmon, or a kimono
or divided skirt of a pure white,
unpatterned material. And when
the actor is a handsome young
man with skin of fine texture and
cheeks glowing with the freshness
of youth, his good looks emerge as
perfection, with a seductive charm
quite different from a woman's.
Here, one sees, is the beauty that
made feudal lords lose themselves
over their boy favorites.

The legendary Shintomiza kabuki theatre, seen from
two angles, the upper one being a view into the
packed house with the roof imaginatively removed.
The Shintomiza was destroyed in the 1923 earth-
quake and fires.

Mobs celebrate one of the many Ichikawa Danjuros,
the most famous Kabuki lineage, at the Shintomiza,
circa 1880

Wriggling Away in Kagurazaka

A Fish...

From Botchan *by Natsume Soseki, 1906*

... once when I was a boy I caught three silver carp in the fishing-pond at Koume in Tokyo. On another occasion—it was at a fair held in front of the Bishamon shrine in the Zenkokuji temple in Kagurazaka—I managed to hook a carp about eight inches long, but just when I thought I had it, it fell back into the water with a splash. I still have a sense of disappointment when I think about it, even now.

A view from Yotsuya Station toward Kagurazaka, circa 1911

The main street ascending Kagurazaka hill at the turn of the 20th century

The commercial center of Asakusa at the turn of the 20th century, with the 'Asakusa 12 Storeys', the Ryounkaku, in the background

These villages and their people all appear identical. So no matter how far you walk you seem to remain where you started, going nowhere at all. And wherever you are in Tokyo you lose your way.

Abe Kobo (1924 - 1993), writer, playwright and painter

. . . And Another Escapee

From The Thieves *by Kawatake Mokuami, 1881*

Shimazo: You asked me to go somewhere with you tonight. Whose house are we going to?

Senta: To a house below Kagurazaka. The man who lives there used to be one of the direct retainers of the Shogunate. He now calls himself a teacher of calligraphy. He's a low dog who can't be trusted. Even before the collapse of the Shogunate he was dismissed for his outrageous intimidation of the people, but he got pardoned in the general amnesty after the Restoration. Since then he has been lending money—stolen money, for all I know. He's a very prosperous gentleman now, and he goes by the name of Mochizuki Akira. I intend to break in there tonight, kill him and his wife, and clean out all his money. Then I'll head for Osaka.

Shimazo: I happen to know something about this Mochizuki. He certainly has money, but you could get it by just threatening him. Why must you kill him and his wife?

Senta: I have my reasons.

Shimazo: What reasons could you have for killing them?

Senta: The woman Mochizuki now publicly recognizes as his wife was until April of this year a famous geisha in Shirakawa. I was so madly in love with her that sometimes I would stay with her ten days running. I spent a fortune trying to get her to give in to me, but she had her sights trained on higher targets, and wouldn't listen to me.

Clam-digging at low tide in Tokyo Bay, circa 1920

93

A Decade of Demonstrations

The terms of the Treaty of Portsmouth, ending the Russo-Japanese War (1904-1905), which the Japanese had won decisively, infuriated many residents of Tokyo, who thought Russia gained more than it deserved. Crowds first gathered at Hibiya Park to protest and, when they were refused entry, rioted throughout the city in what became known as the Hibiya Incendiary Incident, destroying buildings and police boxes. Nearly 20 died.

A police box overturned

Soldiers garrisoned in Hibiya Park, 1905

Protests against various perceived injustices continued about once per year in Tokyo, for more than a decade, in what's come to be called The Era of Popular Violence, culminating in the Rice Riots of 1918, spawned by a drastic increase in the price of rice.

Protestors and police in front of the House of Representatives in 1913

Buddhist monks from a temple in Ginza march toward Kyobashi in support of poor people's need for rice, during the Rice Riots of 1918.

Easy and Comfortable

From Hanabi *(Fireworks) by Nagai Kafu, 1919 (translation from Seidensticker's* Low City, High City, *1983)*

I turned into a side street and noted that the rows of geisha houses were silent, their shutters closed and their lights out. Back on the main street, I was passing time in a beer hall when a young man who seemed to be a student told me of attacks on Ginza shops and on geisha establishments in the Shimbashi area.

The government distributes rice to Tokyo citizens in response to the Rice Riots.

So I first learned of riots over the price of rice. From the next day there were no newspaper reports in the matter. I heard later that the rioting always occurred in the cool of the evening. There was a good moon every evening during those days. Hearing that the rioters gathered menacingly before the houses of the wealthy when the evening had turned cool and the moon had come up, I could not put down a feeling that there was something easy and comfortable about it all. It went on for five or six days and then things returned to normal. On the night of the return to normal, it rained.

The Winds of Spring

From The Romaji Diary *by Ishikawa Takuboku, 1909*

This morning a violent west wind was roaring through the sky. The windows on the third floor were all rattling, and a dustlike sand from the street below came blowing in the cracks. But in spite of the wind the scattered clouds were motionless.

A springlike sunshine was warming the windowpanes. It was the sort of day when you might be sweating if it weren't for the wind. The old man from the lending library came in, wiping his nose with the palm of his hand. "Terrible wind," said he. "Still, the cherry blossoms all over Tokyo will be opening today. Wind or no wind, it's fine weather."

"Spring has come at last," I said, but of course he couldn't understand my feelings.

A Contentious Shrine

Originally built to commemorate those who had fought against the Shogunate in the Boshin War (1868-1869), Yasukuni Shrine gained its present name in 1879. Yasukuni became (in)famous more recently, with the 'enshrinement' in 1978 of 14 people convicted as Class A war criminals from World War II, including Tojo Hideki, as convicted in the The International Military Tribunal for the Far East (IMTFE), commonly referred to as the Tokyo Trials (1946 – 1948). Exhibits on the grounds extol the Japanese military during that war, and Justice Radha Binod Pal of the Trials, who wrote a strong dissenting opinion against what he saw as 'victors' justice', though not doubting that the Japanese military committed atrocities on a massive scale.

Yasukuni during cherry blossom season, circa 1910

Yasukuni—It's Well Worth a Special Trip

From The Thieves *by Kawatake Mokuami, 1881*
First Pilgrim: Who is honored at this shrine?

Noodle Seller: The men who died in the wars. It was for the Emperor's sake that they died, even the soldiers of humble birth, and that's why it has been made so impressive.

Second Pilgrim: I've always gone by without ever looking inside, but it really looks pretty when you see it this way.

Noodle Seller: You should have a look at it by day. There are fountains in the ponds, and the trees in the garden are something to see. Flowers bloom all year round. It's well worth a special trip to see it, even if you come a long way.

A Cult of Violent Patriotism

From My Japanese Holiday *by Maurice Dekobra, 1936*
One can say that no other nation has followed such an ascending curve in so short a time. No white race possesses a Yasukuni jinja, that temple devoted to absolute nationalism or the cult of violent patriotism which inflames all those who feel honoured to die for their country. Individualism, that poison which looks upon each individual of the nation as a living entity, has never gnawed at the Japanese.

Elementary school students in the Yushima district of Tokyo revering the emperor, circa 1900

The Imperial Rescript on Education

Know ye, Our subjects:

Our Imperial Ancestors have founded Our Empire on a basis broad and everlasting and have deeply and firmly implanted virtue; Our subjects ever united in loyalty and filial piety have from generation to generation illustrated the beauty thereof. This is the glory of the fundamental character of Our Empire, and herein also lies the source of Our education.

Ye, Our subjects, be filial to your parents, affectionate to your brothers and sisters; as husbands and wives be harmonious, as friends true; bear yourselves in modesty and moderation; extend your benevolence to all; pursue learning and cultivate arts, and thereby develop intellectual faculties and perfect moral powers; furthermore advance public good and promote common interests; always respect the Constitution and observe the laws; should emergency arise, offer yourselves courageously to the State; and thus guard and maintain the prosperity of Our Imperial Throne coeval with heaven and earth.

So shall ye not only be Our good and faithful subjects, but render illustrious the best traditions of your forefathers. The Way here set forth is indeed the teaching bequeathed by Our Imperial Ancestors, to be observed alike by Their Descendants and the subjects, infallible for all ages and true in all places. It is Our wish to lay it to heart in all reverence, in common with you, Our subjects, that we may thus attain to the same virtue.

Signed by Mutsuhito, the Meiji emperor, on 30 October 1890

A Tokyo kindergarten, 1911

Meiji Constitution

On 11 February 1899 (the anniversary of the day on which the mythical first emperor, Jimmu, was said to have ascended to the throne) the Meiji emperor pressed his seal on Japan's first-ever constitution, Prussian-inspired and drafted by a committee headed by Ito Hirobumi. Features included the right of foreigners to settle elsewhere in the city.

From Commentary on the Constitution of the Empire of Japan, *by Ito Hirobumi, 1906*
The Sacred Throne was established at the time when the heavens and the earth became separated. The Emperor is Heaven descended, divine, and sacred. He is preeminent above all his subjects. He must be reverenced and is inviolable. He has indeed to pay due respect to the law, but the law has no power to hold him accountable to it . . . he shall not be made a topic of derogatory comment nor one of discussion.

Hirohito in 1901 at age one. He would become the Showa emperor in 1926.

Leeches

There are three leeches who suck the people's blood: the emperor, the rich and the big landholders. . . . The Big Bullock of the present government, the emperor, is not the son of the gods as your primary school teachers and others would have you believe. The ancestors of the present emperor came forth from a corner of Kyushu, killing and robbing people as they did. . . . It should be readily obvious that the emperor is not a god if you but think about it for a moment.

When it is said that the [imperial dynasty] has continued for 2,500 years, it may seem as if [the present emperor] is divine, but down through the ages the emperors have been tormented by foreign opponents and, domestically, treated as puppets by their own vassals. . . . Although this is well-known, university professors and their students, weaklings that they are, refuse to either say or write anything about it. Instead, they attempt to deceive both others and themselves, knowing all along the whole thing is a pack of lies.

Two others executed as a result of the Kotoku Incident: anarcho-syndicalist leader Kotoku Denjiro (right) and his paramour Kanno Sugako.

Uchiyama Gudo, a Zen Buddhist priest, writing shortly before he was captured, tried and executed for alleged complicity in the Kotoku Incident of 1911, an anarchist plot to assassinate the emperor. The government used the incident as a pretext to round up dozens they didn't care for, and execute 12, most on circumstantial evidence. In 1993, Uchiyama's Zen sect restored his status as a priest, saying, "when viewed by today's standards of respect for human rights, Uchiyama Gudo's writings contain elements that should be regarded as farsighted".

Signs of Western influence, 1900

Tokyo Stock Exchange, 1920

The End of Meiji

Mutsuhito, the Meiji emperor, died on 29 July 1912, after 45 years on the throne. These particular five decades marked astonishing transitions for Tokyoites and the country's citizens in general, a scope of transformation to be seen again during the six decades that Mutsuhito's grandson, Hirohito, would be on the throne.

From the New York Times *report of the funeral, 13 October 1912*
The contrast between that which preceded the funeral car and that which followed it was striking indeed. Before it went old Japan; after it came new Japan. New Japan quickly separated itself to the left and right and seated itself in the pavilions on either side. But old Japan had passed by and disappeared, and we could only hear now and again the distant wail of the reed pipes.

Facing the imperial palace in July 1912, when the Meiji emperor's death was announced

The funeral procession

A high-fashion hairstyle of the period, here sported by geisha, the '203 Kouchi' (Hill 203) was named after a hill in Port Arthur, China, which was the location of a major battle in the Russo-Japanese war – suitably, the hairdo is piled up high. The Japanese lost more than 10,000 troops conquering the hill, about 15% of total losses in the war, including the remaining son of General Nogi Maresuke.

A teahouse garden

The Greatest Nation in the World

From What Shall I Think of Japan? *by George Gleason (head of YMCA Japan for 16 years), 1921*

An English teacher new to Japan, wishing to start some interesting conversation, asked his class: "What is needed to make Japan great?" A student promptly raised his hand, and when called on replied: "Sir, Japan already is the greatest nation in the world."

"The war office, in maintaining its own foreign policy, is bringing evil consequences upon the Empire."
The Tokyo Asahi newspaper, 1919

Following In His Lord's Footsteps

General Nogi Maresuke, a national hero after the Phyrric victory over Russia in the Russo-Japanese War (1904 –1905), later headed the Peers School, becoming a lead tutor for the young Hirohito, who would become the Showa emperor (1926 – 1989). In the passage below, Viscount Kaneko Kentaro reflects, years later, on the events surrounding the Meiji emperor's funeral in 1912.

In the assault on Port Arthur, some thirty thousand Japanese soldiers gave up their lives. This sacrifice of life was at first much criticized in Japan, but public sentiment changed in face of the fact that the General lost both his sons. He returned to Japan a victor, it is true, but a most unhappy man. Always in his mind were thoughts of the families of the thirty thousand brave young men it had been necessary to sacrifice. He did not want to be acclaimed in the streets, but to be let alone. He went about in an old uniform and tried to be as inconspicuous as possible.

One day at an audience with the Emperor Meiji, Nogi said to him as he was leaving, something to the effect that he should never see him again. The Emperor, gathering that Nogi was contemplating seppuku, called him back.

"Nogi," he said, "I still have need of you. I want your life."

So the General did not carry out his plan at that time, but lived on, as the Emperor had ordered him to do, becoming president of the school at which the sons of nobles are educated. All through the years, however, he was haunted by the memory of the thirty thousand soldiers he had been compelled to send to their death.

When the Emperor Meiji died, Nogi was one of the guard of honour, made up of peers, who in rotation watched at the Imperial bier for forty days and forty nights.

Then came the state funeral. On the day of the funeral Nogi wrote a poem which declared in effect, "I shall follow in the footsteps of Your Majesty." This poem he showed to Prince Yamagata, who took it to mean merely that Nogi

Viscount Kaneko Kentaro, circa 1920

would be in the procession following the Imperial remains to the grave.

But when the guns announced the departure of the funeral cortege from the palace, Nogi was not there. Like the samurai of old, he desired to follow his dead master into the beyond. At the sound of the guns he took his short sword and committed seppuku, while in the next room Countess Nogi, his devoted wife, dressed all in white, cut the arteries of her neck. Thus the two died together, for the sake of the Emperor and the thirty thousand soldiers who had sacrificed their lives.

Nogi's death testimonial, translation from Legends of the Samurai *by Hiroaki Sato, 1995*
In committing suicide to follow His Majesty in death, I am aware, with regret, that my crime in doing so is by no means negligible. However, since I lost my flag during the civil war of the tenth year of Meiji [1877], I have been looking for an appropriate opportunity to die, to no avail. Instead, to this day I have continued to be showered with imperial special favors and treated with exceptional compassion. While I have grown infirm, with few days left to be useful, this grave event has filled me with such remorse that I hereby have made this decision.

The house where General Nogi and his wife committed seppuku *(him) and* jigai *(her) is preserved at Nogizaka ('Nogi's hill') in downtown Tokyo, several minutes' walk from Roppongi Station.*

The Nihonbashi district at the time of the Meiji emperor's death

The Birth of Tokyo Station

From Mysterious Japan *by Julian Street, 1921*
The central railroad station exhibits the capital's modern architectural trend. It is conveniently arranged and impressive in its magnitude as seen across the open space on which it faces, but there its merit stops. Like most large foreign-style buildings in Japan, it is architecturally an ugly thing. Standing at the gate of Japan's chief city, it has about it nothing Japanese. Its façade is grandiose and meaningless, and as one turns one's back upon it and sees other large new public structures, one is saddened by the discovery that the Japanese, skillful at adaptation though they have often shown themselves, have signally failed to adapt the requirements, methods, and materials of modern building to their old national architectural lines. One thing is certain, however: there will be no new public buildings more unsightly than those already standing. This style of architecture in Japan has touched bottom.

In twenty years or so I believe the ugliness of these modern piles will have become apparent to the Japanese. It will dawn upon them that they need not go to Europe and America for architectural themes, but to the castle of Nagoya, the watchtowers above the moat of the Imperial Palace, the palace gates, and the temples and pagodas everywhere.

Panorama of Tokyo Station, at the time of its opening in 1914

Filled with Rapture

From Terry's Guide to the Japanese Empire *by T. Philip Terry, 1914*

After dark Tokyo is a big dusky village to all but the initiated, and to some an intolerably dull one. Unless one figures in the diplomatic swing, and officiates at the almost ceaseless round of entertainments enjoyed by that favored class, there is little for the average man to do outside the comfortable hotel; the few thousand foreigners who dwell in Tokyo are practically lost in the huge metropolis. On the other hand, the Japanese, who do not go in much for a fast life, and who are easily pleased, find the decorous allurements of Tokyo so potent that they are drawn to them, as by magnets, from all parts of the Empire. To hobnob perpetually with a tiny pot of insipid, sugarless tea and a tobacco-pipe with a bowl no bigger than bullet, the while listening to the beating of a tom-tom and the doleful ditties of pantomimic geisha, fills them with rapture; and once installed in the capital they regard with positive pity those who are so unfortunate as to dwell outside it.

The Interim Emperor

Yoshihito, the cerebrally challenged Taisho emperor, nominally held the throne from 1912 to 1926. Edward Behr, author of Hirohito: Behind the Mask *(1989) describes Yoshihito's 'futile' existence, passion for Gothic iconography and the building of a miniature Versailles, Tokyo's Akasaka Palace (today the State Guesthouse, residence of state leaders for APEC summits and the like). According to Behr, Yoshihito's father, the Meiji emperor, "found it in atrocious taste, and only went there once".*

Yoshihito and his son, Hirohito, 1905

'A Homogenous Race Since Antiquity'

From the Kokushi, *written by Shiratori Kurakichi for the education of the young Hirohito and his classmates, 1912 (translation from Hi-*

rohito and the Making of Modern Japan *by Herbert Bix, 2000).* 'Kokutai' *is often translated as 'national polity' – it was a central concept in bolstering facism in the following few decades.*

The imperial house unified our land and people and created the empire. Not only did it rule as the head of state, it also became integrated with the people and the head of their religion. Because of the ineffable feeling of intimacy between the throne and the people, the imperial house was able to create an extremely firm foundation for a state. However, just as the imperial house is a line of emperors unbroken for ages eternal; the people too, from generation to generation, father to child, have propagated down to today. Not once has there been a change in the race. Therefore we, descendants of the people who assisted the founder at the time of her creation of the state, have carried out the will of our ancestors and become eternally loyal subjects. The successive imperial families have loved the loyal subjects of their progenitor and always trusted in the people's cooperation in carrying out their grand plans. This indeed is the essence of our *kokutai* . . . There is no mistake . . . in saying that we have been a homogeneous race since antiquity.

Nothing Curious or Extraordinary About Them

From The Decay of Lying – An Observation *by Oscar Wilde, 1889*

If you set a picture by Hokusai, or Hokkei, or any of the great native painters, beside a real Japanese gentleman or lady, you will see that there is not the slightest resemblance between them. The actual people who live in Japan are not unlike the general run of English people; that is to say, they are extremely commonplace, and have nothing curious or extraordinary about them. In fact the whole of Japan is a pure invention. There is no such country, there are no such people.

. . . and three from a geisha house in 1912 . . .

Three beauties from Hokusai, early 19th century . . .

. . . and three on a Ginza street in 1930

The Rise of The Salaryman

A family on the outskirts of Tokyo receives an unwelcome visitor in 1916, the era of Japan's first flights.

Scholars trace the roots of the 'salaryman' concept back centuries, to a time following the end of the nearly two centuries of civil war that ended in the early 17th century with the establishement of the shogunate, when, gradually, former samurai were forced to take up non-military occupations. The Meiji Restoration (1868), which ended the shogunate, added impetus to this transition. Modern Japanese salarymen often still consider themselves as something like the samurai of their corporate entities.

From I Am A Cat *by Natsume Soseki, 1906*
If one becomes a businessman, one has to get to the top. Anywhere lower on the ladder, you have to go around spouting idiotic flatteries and drinking *sake* with the boss when there's nothing you want

less. Altogether, it's a stupid way of life.

Ever since my school-days I've always taken a scunner to businessmen. They'll do anything for money. They are, after all, what they used to be called in the good old days: the very dregs of society.

Shaky Town

From Fourteen Year of Diplomatic Life in Japan *by Albert d'Anethan, 1912*
While I was sitting with Princess Komatsu we were favored with a shock of earthquake. This was a rather alarming occurrence, as earlier in the morning we had been treated to a very sharp shock. The Princess, however, showed the greatest composure and dignity, never moving from her seat. I felt, therefore, with this splendid example before me of courage and sangfroid (icy nerves), the least I could do was to act likewise, but nevertheless my feelings on this occasion, glued as I was to my chair, are more easily imagined than expressed!

When, after five or six years, you discover that you do not in the least understand the mind of the Japanese, then you will be able to say that you know its chief characteristic.

Lafcadio Hearn (1850 – 1904)

From Japan Weekly Chronicle, *1 January 1920*
A Tokyo factory inspector claimed that by 1918 the number of children under fourteen years of age had been reduced in the Tokyo factories subject to the law from 2,000 to 1,057.

RIGHT: *Members of the Japanese Red Cross leaving Shinbashi Station, bound for France and WWI, 1914*

The fire brigade puts on a show in Hibiya Park, circa 1911

In the Beginning, Woman Was the Sun

In the beginning Woman was the Sun. She was a genuine being. Now Woman is the Moon. She lives through others and glitters through the mastery of others. She has a pallor like that of the ill. Now we must restore our hidden Sun.

With these words echoing the Shinto creation myth, Hiratsuka Raicho founded Seito [Bluestocking], Japan's first literary publication led by women, in 1911, an expression of the dawning women's consciousness movement.

Hiratsuka and other leaders of Japan's early feminist movement forming the New Women's Association in 1920

Knowing the Guards

From The Autobiography of Osugi Sakae, 1920s *(translation by Byron K. Marshall, 1992)*

In Tokyo Jail, where they keep the accused awaiting trial, was an old guard nicknamed Repeaters. Whenever we were summoned to court as defendants, we were lined up along a wide dimly lit corridor before being put together with a dozen or so others into a horse-drawn van (now I suppose the job is done by automobile). In the corridor our hands were shackled in manacles chained to our waists, and roll was called out by the head of the escort section. Then the old guard referred to as Repeaters took over as one of the two escorts for each group. I do not know how long he had been assigned to escort duty or when he had received his nickname. But surely he had been eating prison food for at least thirty years and must have been somewhere close to sixty.

The first edition of Seito, *cover art by Takamura Chieko*

A Publisher's Work is Never Done

Ito Noe reflects on her life as publisher of Seito *after Hiratsuka's departure in 1915*
There is no one to consult. There is no one to whom I can turn for assistance. Recently I have been getting upset and cross even when my good friend Kobayashi Katsu comes to visit me. Somehow I am unable to get used to going out constantly to pick up advertisements and take care of other business, and I always return home completely exhausted. The child is always waiting for me to feed him.

Whenever there's a free moment, I find laundry to do. And then the proofreading. . . . Nevertheless, the thought that I have perhaps helped some other young people encourages me to continue.

Osugi (center) and Seito *publisher Ito (right) were lovers in the last years of their lives. They and his 6-year-old nephew were beaten to death by military police, led by Lieutenant Amakasu Masahiko, in their prison cells in mid September 1923, as part of the attacks on socialists, anarchists, ethnic Koreans and other perceived threats to the increasingly fascist government, following the Great Kanto Earthquake. Amakasu was later one of the leaders of the Japanese subversion of Manchuria, and killed himself by biting a cyanide capsule at war's end in 1945. A character based on his life was played by Sakamoto Ryuichi in Bertolucci's* The Last Emperor *(1987).*

A Royal Visit

The then Prince of Wales, later King Edward VIII (briefly – he famously preferred Wallis Simpson to the crown), visited Tokyo in the spring of 1922.

A bento (boxed meal) sold in Akasaka Station at the time of the Prince's visit

Japan's Nouveau Riche – *Narikin*

From Mysterious Japan *by Julian Street, 1921*

A case in point is the slang term *narikin* which they have recently adopted to describe the flashy new-rich type which has come into being since the war.

To understand the derivation of this word, and its witty con-

Throngs welcome the then Prince of Wales as he leaves Tokyo Station, proceeding under yet another commemorative arch.

notation, you must know that in their game of chess, called *shogi*, a humble pawn advanced to the adversary's third row is, by a process resembling queening, converted into a powerful, free-moving piece called *kin*. The word *nari* means 'to become'; hence *nari-kin* means literally 'to become *kin*'—which gives us, when applied to a flamboyant profiteer, a droll picture of a poor little pawn suddenly exalted to power and magnificence. The pun, which adds greatly to the value of this term, comes with the word *kin*. *Kin* is not only a chessman; it also means 'gold'. Which naturally contributes further piquancy in the application to a *nouveau riche*.

From The Chrysanthemum and the Sword *by Ruth Benedict, 1946*
But it still remains true that the greatest bitterness of Japanese public opinion is turned not against the Zaibatsu but against the *narikin. Narikin* is often translated '*nouveau riche*' but that does not do justice to the Japanese feeling. In the United States *nouveaux riches* are strictly 'newcomers'; they are laughable because they are gauche and have not had time to acquire the proper polish. This liability, however, is balanced by the heartwarming asset that they have come up from the log cabin, they have risen from driving a mule to controlling oil millions. But in Japan a *narikin* is a term taken from Japanese chess and means a pawn promoted to queen. It is a pawn rampaging about the board as a 'big shot'. It has no hierarchal right to do any such thing. The *narikin* is believed to have obtained his wealth by defrauding or exploiting others and the bitterness directed toward him is as far as possible from the attitude in the United States toward the 'home boy who makes good'. Japan provided a place in her hierarchy for great wealth and kept an alliance with it; when wealth is achieved in the field outside, Japanese public opinion is bitter against it.

Liaisons

From The Old Days of the New Theater *by Tanaka Eizo, 1957*
In those days, Toyamagahara was a parade ground covered by thick grasses. I'd heard that Waseda students used the sand pits there to meet with the girls and maids from their rooming houses . . .

A stylish stroller, circa 1955

A Most Unlikely Contingency

James Francis Abbott, "sometimes instructor at the Japanese National Naval Academy," Japanese Expansion and American Policies, *1916*
In this little book, I have attempted to give the facts upon which I base my opinion that war between Japan and America during the present generation is a most unlikely contingency.

Taisho Tokyo

Crown Prince Hirohito returns to Tokyo after a Euro tour, 3 September 1921. Alighting at Tokyo Station, he returned to the palace through welcoming throngs.

A new streetcar line

Taisho-era fashion in Hibiya Park

From The Book of Tea *by Okakura Kakuko, 1906*

Tea began as a medicine and grew into a beverage. In China, in the eighth century, it entered the realm of poetry as one of the polite amusements. The fifteenth century saw Japan ennoble it into a religion of aestheticism — Teaism. Teaism is a cult founded on the adoration of the beautiful among the sordid facts of everyday existence. It inculcates purity and harmony, the mystery of mutual charity, the romanticism of the social order. It is essentially a worship of the Imperfect, as it is a tender attempt to accomplish something possible in this impossible thing we know as life.

...

The long isolation of Japan from the rest of the world, so conducive to introspection, has been highly favourable to the development of Teaism. Our home and habits, costume and cuisine, porcelain, lacquer, painting--our very literature--all have been subject to its influence. No student of Japanese culture could ever ignore its presence. It has permeated the elegance of noble boudoirs, and entered the abode of the humble. Our peasants have learned to arrange flowers, our meanest labourer to offer his salutation to the rocks and waters. In our common parlance we speak of the man "with no tea" in him, when he is insusceptible to the serio-comic interests of the personal drama. Again we stigmatise the untamed aesthete who, regardless of the mundane tragedy, runs riot in the springtide of emancipated emotions, as one "with too much tea" in him.

A teahouse maiden, 1930

The City Destroyed – Again

At two minutes to noon on 1 September 1923, Tokyo was struck by the Great Kanto Earthquake, a 7.9 temblor with its hypocenter about 100 km south of the city. The quake remains in the top ten of the deadliest in known history, claiming something like 140,000 lives. Most died in the subsequent firestorms – many pepople were cooking lunch at the time, and the cooking fires ignited the collapsed wood-built structures. The firestorms created such intense heat that streets melted, so those fleeing burning houses sunk into the molten tar, or were par-boiled if they jumped into the super-heated Sumida River. The fires burned for two days. Nearly 40,000 died in one location of supposed refuge, the yard of the military Clothing Depot, which was engulfed by a firestorm, fueled by the blankets and clothing the refugees had brought.

Devastated Asakusa – in the background stands the former 12-story Ryounkaku, now down to eight.

A flattened Marunouchi, the business center of the city . . .

. . . and a burning post office

EARTHQUAKE FIRE DESTROYED GREATER PART OF TOKYO. THOR-
OUGHGOING RECONSTRUCTION NEEDED. PLEASE COME IMMEDI-
ATELY, IF POSSIBLE, EVEN FOR SHORT TIME.

*A cable from Japan Home Minister Goto Shinpei to Charles Beard, a friend and a U.S.
civil administrator. Beard's reply:*

LAY OUT NEW STREETS, FORBID BUILDING WITHOUT STREET-LINES,
UNIFY RAILWAY STATIONS.

Thousands with nowhere else to go set up camp in the broad flat grounds in front of the Imperial Palace.

Having lost homes and livelihood, many fled Tokyo after the quake.

From Tokyo Year Zero *by David Peace, 2007 — a fictionalization in first-person of a Japanese detective's pursuit of a mass murderer immediately post-war — this passage describes his initial arrival in the city twenty years earlier*

I came here the day after the Great Kanto Earthquake; that day the whole city stank, stank of rotten apricots, and the closer I walked to Asakusa and to the winds that blew across from the east of the river, the stronger the stink of the apricots became . . . the stink of rotten apricots that was the stench of the dead, the mountains of dead lain out under a burning sky among the charred ruins on both banks of the Sumida . . . I stood among those corpses piled up high along the riverbanks and the body of one young boy it caught my eye, his body caked black in rags and filth, his face and hands covered in blisters and boils . . .

Ethnic Koreans rounded up following rumors that they'd been looting and poisoning wells following the quake. Thousands died in these attacks by roaming, enraged bands, sometimes supported by police.

A postcard promoting reconstruction – 'Rebuilding a Great Tokyo'

The downtown Kanda district well under way to restoration, late 1923

The Hotel That Survived

HOTEL STANDS
UNDAMAGED AS A
MONUMENT
OF YOUR GENIUS
[STOP]
HUNDREDS OF HOMELESS
PROVIDED BY PERFECTLY
MAINTAINED SERVICE
[STOP]
CONGRATULATIONS
[STOP]

Cable from Okura Kihachiro, one of the shareholders of Tokyo's Imperial Hotel, to architect Frank Lloyd Wright.

From My Japanese Holiday *by Maurice Dekobra, 1936*
Fujita came to me in the hall of the Imperial Hotel. The most palatial hotel in Tokio, which has only one story and is like a bathing establishment with its maze of narrow passages, its comfortable rooms with low ceilings and narrow loophole windows. This bizarre architecture is necessary in a country so often subject to earthquakes. The proof is that the Imperial Hotel came unscathed out of the catastrophe of 1923.

The hotel actually suffered substantial damage, but Wright's having eagerly passed Okura's cable to journalists established the canard as

Months after the quake, people were still living rough in downtown – here's a shot of daily life in Ueno Park in spring 1924.

a common assumption.

Another Hotel in the Offing

From Belli Looks at Life and Law in Japan *by Melvin Belli, 1960*

The Imperial Hotel is at the crossroads of Tokyo, indeed of Japan, and in its bars no doubt were hatched, concocted and mixed many of the great Oriental political, economic and romantic, as the case may be, plots of modern times. The cuisine of the immaculate dining room and

the cosmopolitan service of the back grill lend themselves to intrigue and romance, as well as splendid dining, depending upon the gastronomic or mental impetus of the patron. Although the Imperial has recently been extended toward the railroad tracks, it's generally filled; renewed discussion of a 750-room $15,000,000 Tokyo Hilton Hotel is heard.

From The Autobiography of Osugi Sakae, *1920s (translation by Byron K. Marshall, 1992)*

I don't know how matters are arranged now, but in that period almost all the private middle schools in Tokyo held entrance examinations for every grade in each school term of the year. Thus their practice was to gather applicants two or three times at the beginning of each term, give them entrance examinations, and collect the examination fee each time. This was the third and last time of the year for both Junten and Tokyo Middle School to take applicants.

Somehow, I thought, I had to enter the one or the other. But the two tests were to be held at almost the same time. I had sufficient confidence in my scholastic abilities, but in order not to run the slightest risk I decided to have someone take the test at the Junten Middle School for me . . .

I failed the [Tokyo] test. My stand-in, however, did quite well, answering every question, and passed. So, thanks to him, I entered the fifth-year class at Junten Middle School.

Working Men, Women and ... Kids

From What Shall I Think of Japan? *by George Gleason, 1921*

The factory laws in force from 1 September 1916 have been cynically criticized as "solely for the benefit of the Westerner. Being tired of telling curious visiting foreigners that Japan had no labor laws, they put some on the statute-book and suspended their execution for the most part. The former fact is advertised, and the latter concealed unless the visitor is unusually inquisitive."

In 1917 The Yomiuri newspaper in Tokyo published a brochure describing no less than sixty-five different occupations in which women were engaged. Besides the million female operatives in factories, the Tokyo daily found 4,000 working for the Government Railway and 6,000 in the Tobacco Monopoly Bureau. Women are working in the banks, at the telephones, in the retail stores, and at the typewriter. Women journalists, women novelists, and women doctors and social workers are rapidly increasing.

Celebrants of universal (male) suffrage. The character '普' on display on the side of the car means, in this case, 'widespread'.

More Stirring Times Ahead

A letter to George Gleason from a Japanese friend, 1920
In the meantime Ozaki shouts for universal suffrage and the Young Men's Reconstruction Society of Tokyo conducts a big parade, while the mob that tries to get into the UMCA auditorium to hear the speeches nearly wrecks the building. These are stirring times with prospects of more stirring ones ahead.

RIGHT AND BOTTOM: Posters promoting voting in the first election (1928) open to all males age 25 and over. In the lower one, the dark left side with few people queuing says, 'if you give up your right, darkness' the brighter right side with lots of people queuing says, 'if you vote, brightness'.

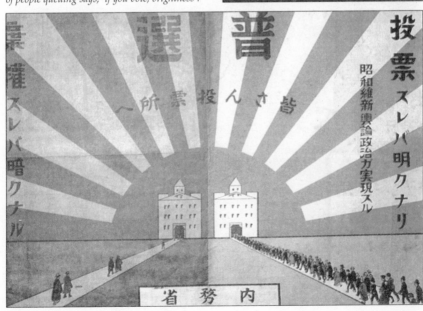

Japan Datapoints – 1927, 1960 and now

	1927	1960	2010
Population (millions)	61	93	128
Children per family	4.2 (1940)	2.8	2
Suicides (% of population)	0.2%	0.2%	0.25%
Divorce (% of population)	1%	1%	2%
Average age at marriage (men)	27		31
Average age at marriage (women)	23		29
Starting salary for government officials (month)	¥75		¥300,000
Cigarettes (one pack)	¥0.15		¥400
Coffee (one cup)	¥0.1		¥400
Large draft beer	¥0.42		¥400

New Lifestyles

The Aoyama Apartment complex, built after the 1923 earthquake and specifically offering Western-style, earthquake- and fire-resistant construction, near today's Harajuku Station. It was mostly destroyed with the building of Omotesando Hills in 2005.

From Mirror, Sword and Jewel *by Kurt Singer, who lived in Tokyo and Sendai in the 1930s.*

In modern Japan the history of municipal administration was largely a chronicle of corruption and bribery, often following a pattern all too familiar in the West. The amorphous character of Tokyo's streets, except in the immediate neighborhood of the old Shogun's castle (now the Imperial Palace), is symbolic of the true nature of the Japanese city, a cluster of villages grown to immoderate dimensions.

A new phenomenon in the early 1920s,
roman *(romance) magazines*

*Western building, Western food – but still
sitting* seiza *style, heels tucked under bums*

*Massively popular new electric heaters of the
late 1920s*

*The first subway in Asia, the Ginza Line,
welcomed its first passengers on 1 January
1928. Would-be passengers queued for more
than an hour for an initial ride, and dressed
up for the occasion.*

Crowded

Kumagaya Tokuichi discusses his Tokyo abode in the 1930s (quoted in Japan At War *by Haruko and Theodore Cook, 1992). Seven and a half mats is roughly 15 square meters – the space covered by two cars parked side-by-side.*

Our family lived in one of the many row houses in Tokyo. The house had two small rooms: one was four-and-a-half mats in area, the other just three. It was really crowded—my parents, three elder sisters, one elder brother, a younger brother, and me all packed in.

Celebrating a Birth

From My Japanese Holiday *by Maurice Dekobra, 1936*

I reached Tokio in December. Her Majesty the Empress had just given birth to the Crown Prince. A son had been born in the palace, and the arrival filled the whole nation with delight. Japanese journalists, who had given me a hearty welcome at Kobe, roused me that morning about eight o'clock to inform me of the good news. Still half-asleep I was urged to express my satisfaction at this happy event. This enthusiastic ringing up on the telephone is now a Japanese custom. For one can hardly imagine a Parisian journalist telephoning to a foreign visitor at daybreak to tell him with deep emotion that the President of the Republic has just become a proud father.

That day five hundred thousand children from the Tokio schools, boys and girls, from seven to fifteen years of age, marched past the front of the famous temple. It was an imposing symbolical spectacle, which could not fail to inspire the most indifferent with salutary reflections. Each section of the children was led by a master or professor, generally a little man with spectacles or pince-nez, wearing a black coat and grey striped trousers.

As they halted in front of the sanctuary, the schoolmaster stepped forward three paces, bowed low three times, imitated by the children, who followed his lead. Then the procession went on, now in the direction of the Imperial park where hundreds of thousands of children waved their little flags and without even seeing the palace, acclaimed him in front of a wall behind which was the building where the little baby lay. This was the Son of God on earth, appointed to guide later on his people along the path of Eternal Triumph.

Students listening to a national radio broadcast, 1935

In 1930, the Tsubame *express train reduced travel time between Tokyo and Osaka by two hours, to about eight.*

Clever Promotion

Sugai Toshiko reminisces about her adolescent career in the theater in the 1930s (quoted in Japan At War *by Haruko and Theodore Cook, 1992).*
The Moulin Rouge building was three stories high. On the roof was a red windmill with turning blades. There weren't many tall buildings then, except for a few department stores like Mitsukoshi, so you could see it clear across town at night. It was a Tokyo landmark. When it opened in 1931, you couldn't advertise like you can today, so Mother and Father went to the baseball stadium and paged themselves: "Will Mr. Takanawa of the Shinjuku Moulin Rouge please return to your theater immediately?" When we went to the public bath, they'd tell everybody,"The show running at the Moulin is really funny."

Although things were going great, we had a premonition of what was coming. Censorship of the scripts grew stricter and we couldn't throw in ad libs as freely. We had to reserve a special seat right in the middle of the theater for the policeman. If he declared, "No further!" we had to shut the curtain and stop the play.

Wasting Electricity

From In Praise of Shadows *by Tanizaki Jun'ichiro, 1933*
The novelist Takebayashi Musoan said when he returned from Paris a few years ago that Tokyo and Osaka were far more brightly lit than any European city; that even on the Champs Élysées there were still houses lit by oil lamps, while in Japan hardly a one remained unless in a remote mountain village. Perhaps no two countries in the world waste more electricity than America and Japan, he said, for Japan is only too anxious to imitate America in every way it can. That was some four or five years ago, before the vogue for neon signs. Imagine his surprise were he to come home today, when everything is so much brighter.

Medieval Minds

From Political and Strategic Implications of the Far East Situation, *Col. Gary I. Crockett, 1938*
In a few decades Japan was thus transformed from a feudal to a modern state. But the inherent traits and mentality of the people were not changed. We have, therefore, the presence among the family of nations of a people fully equipped with modern appliances for making war and skillful in their use, but with a medieval mind. And these people believe that all their greatness has come from war.

The Stream of Japanese Life

From Mirror, Sword and Jewel *by Kurt Singer, who lived in Tokyo and Sendai in the 1930s.*

Seeing the Japanese mother in the street, serenely sauntering and humming, with her child attached to her back, one feels that it is through her that the stream of Japanese life runs and refreshes itself. The over-busy and excessively self-conscious males appear, compared to her, a mere protuberance, unattractive and lacking authenticity; useful or noisome instruments, hardly initiated in the mystery of being.

RIGHT: *Hitomi Kinue (left – note the rising sun graphic above her number), the Babe Didrikson of Japan, held some world records and was the first Japanese woman to win an Olympic medal. She's shown here finishing second in the women's 800m in Amsterdam in 1928.*

BOTTOM LEFT: *U.S. baseball stars Lou Gehrig and Babe Ruth visit Japan in 1932 to celebrate the launch of the country's professional baseball league.*

BOTTOM RIGHT: *Charlie Chaplin visited too in the same year – he became the target of an assassination plot by fascists who didn't care for his politics.*

What Should We Wear?

From Daughter of the Pacific *by Matsuoka Yoko, 1952*
Mother's habit of wearing Western dresses apparently displeased His Excellency, for he told Father it was a disgrace and that Mother should be wearing kimonos. However, Mother never yielded to this fancy, and Father stuck by his stubborn wife. Perhaps this was an expression of their protest against a ruthless and rigid society. When I realize how inconsequential this sort of resistance was, in proportion to the risk involved — for it could have resulted in Father's discharge — I become acutely aware of the immense power which the rulers exercised under such a social system.

From The True Face of Japan *by Nohara Komakichi, 1936*
Not ten Japanese women in a hundred, not five, not even two, wear European dress, although this is much cheaper and perhaps more convenient than the native kimono. At the most one in a hundred wears European dress, and this only in the large towns. We are not particularly proud of the 'modern girls' in European dress, who are somewhat contemptuously called 'compact girls' by the populace, in reference to the 'compact powder' which the girls publicly dab on their faces upon every available occasion.

The moga ('modern gal') hairstyle above kimono, circa 1930

Moga *setting out for a drive, late 1920s*

The Western woman adorns herself with furs, because she is so closely akin to the brute beasts that she wears their skins on her back. These animals are her brothers.

Magazine article in the early 1930s

Varieties of women's attire in the mid 1930s

The goldfish mart

A May Day protest in Tokyo in 1930

Uno Chiyo, famed editor of Style *magazine and author of* Confessions of Love *and* Ohan *(made into a massively popular movie in the 1980s) at her desk in 1936, sporting the popular* moga *hairstyle. Uno's, er, non-traditional lifestyle (a dozen houses, easily as many husbands and lovers, tax evasion and bankruptcy) routinely scandalized city residents of the time. One biography claims that, when she first bobbed her hair in 1927, the children of the neighborhood ran away in fright. At 86, she published a best-selling autobiographical anthem,* I Will Keep Living, *which title proved prophetic. A resident of the city's Minato Ward for decades, she died in her house near Aoyama Blvd. in 1996, two years shy of her 100th birthday.*

Advertisement for a train's dining car, 1936

Hachiko, the most famous dog in Japan, was adopted by Ueno Hidesaburo in 1924. Hachiko daily accompanied Ueno, an agricultural scientist on faculty at Tokyo Imperial University (now the University of Tokyo) to Tokyo's Shibuya Station, where Ueno would board the train to go to work. Hachiko then waited for Ueno to return at the end of the day. In 1925, Ueno died suddenly during a lecture at the University, and therefore didn't return. Hachiko continued to visit the station daily and wait for Ueno – for nine years, until he died there, on 8 March 1935. The Hachiko statue on the west side of the JR Shibuya Station is perhaps the most famous meeting place in today's Tokyo. Hachiko's stuffed carcass remains on display at the National Science Museum in Ueno. One version of the oft-told story is the 2009 movie Hachiko: A Dog's Story, set in the United States and starring Richard Gere.

A pet shop

Kao shampoo debuted in 1932.

Kagome tomato juice debuted in 1933. The six-pointed star isn't a Star of David, it's an ancient Shinto symbol. Similar case with what Westerners know commonly as the swastika, which is an ancient Hindu and Buddhist symbol.

Celebrating the fall of Nanjing to the Japanese occupation forces – Ginza, December 1937

Bullfight of Love

Durng a lovely mid May day in Tokyo's southern district of Shinagawa in 1936, the city police burst into a woman's hotel room. She declared that she was Abé Sada, whom they had been seeking since the news of a gruesome murder a few days earlier that had caused a national sensation and at least one panic, in Ginza. When the police weren't convinced by Abé's statement, as Mark Schreiber has it in The Dark Side: *'she produced a piece of light brown paper from her bodice and opened it to display an unmistakable piece of evidence linking her to the crime.'*

Abé Sada arrested

From Japanese Portraits: Pictures of Different People *by Donald Richie, 1987*
After the war, released from prison, she got herself a job in Inari-cho, in downtown Tokyo: at the Hoshi-Kiku-Sui—the Star-Chrysanthemum-Water—a pub.

There, every night, workers of the neighborhood—for it was a *taishu-saka-ba*, a workingman's pub—would gather to drink saké and shochu and nibble grilled squid and pickled radish. And every night around ten, Sada Abé would make her entrance.

It was grand. She descended the staircase—itself a large affair which ended right in the middle of the customers. Always in bright kimono, one redolent of the time of her crime, early Showa, 1936, Sada Abé would appear at the head of the stairs, stop, survey the crowd below, and then slowly descend.

From where, one never knew. Some said that her lair was up there on the second floor, full of old photographs and overstuffed furniture. Others said that the staircase went nowhere at all, that she had to clamber up it from the back before she could arrive in public. In any event, the descent was dramatic, with many pauses as she stared at her guests below, turning a brief gaze on this one and that. And as she did so, progressing slowly, indignation was expressed.

It always appeared. It was part of the show, the entrance. Ostensibly it was provoked by the actions of the men below. They invariably placed their hands over their privates. Fingers squeezed tight, they would then turn and snicker. Above, the descending Sada Abé would mime fury, casting burning glances at those below who squeezed and giggled the more. She slapped the banister in her wrath, and merriment rippled.

This pantomime was occasioned by the nature of Sada Abé's crime. Twenty years before, she had cut off her lover's penis. This was after he was dead, of course. And he was dead because the two had discovered that if she squeezed his neck hard enough his weary member achieved new life, but one day she squeezed too hard and killed him.

LEFT: *Abé at her mirror, preparing for her work at the pub, 1950s*

RIGHT: *A still from* Ai No Korida *['Bullfight of Love'], a cinematic retelling of the love affair between Abé and the disfigured-in-death Ishida Kichizo. Unusually graphic for its time with unsimulated sexual activity,* Ai No Korida *was widely censured in Japan on its release in 1976. The actress playing Abé Sada, Matsuda Eiko, eventually fled Japan for Paris because of harsh domestic reaction to the film, titled* In The Realm of the Senses *for Western audiences. Quincy Jones recorded a hit pop song with the name* Ai No Corrida *in 1981.*

141

Big Guys

Okada Shogi commenting in the late 18th century on a sumo match

The ring is made of sixteen rice bales. One each for the points of the compass and each of the twelve months. A bale is removed from each side for an entrance. Two huge men entered the ring and bowed in the direction of a Lord, the sponsor. An official with a wand-like fan of office followed them. The wrestlers were amazingly fat, with great flanks and arms, bulging buttocks and cheeks like hanging melons. They wear ritual aprons of costly materials and they rinsed their mouths from buckets of water. The biggest one was the champion. He was called the *yokozuna*, leader of the *makunouchi* — 'ones-within-the-curtain'.

The *dohyoiri*, the ring entry ceremony, began. The ceremony of the entry of the wrestlers was impressive. The wrestlers stamping their feet, throwing some grains of salt, clapping their hands and bowing to the sponsor, the official, and the guests. The ceremony over, the two large men faced each other, their aprons off, wearing loin cloths, their large hands out, knees bent, their little eyes almost lost in fat. Then, with a grunt, they met, struggled for grips, locked limbs, grunted, heaved and panted. There are 48 different falls and throws. The men must stay within those accepted forms.

The Streak

Starting on 7 January 1936, Futabayama (born Akiyoshi Sadaji) won 69 consecutive bouts, a record that stands today. Japan was captivated by the streak, which began with Futabayama ranked as a sekiwake and ended on 3 January 1939, by which time he had achieved the highest rank, yokozuna.

Futabayama prepares for the final match of his streak.

Ironically, he endorsed a stomach medicine, but his streak was broken in part because he was suffering from dysentery.

The iconic candy brand Glico started including trinkets in their product boxes in 1929, mimicking Cracker Jack in the USA. The one shown top left is a bas-relief of Saigo Takamori, the 'Last Samurai'.

143

Intoxication in Various Forms

From Mysterious Japan *by Julian Street, 1921*
I had heard that *sake* was extremely intoxicating, but that is not so. It is rice wine, almost white in colour, and is served sometimes at normal temperature and sometimes slightly warm. It is rather more like a pale light sherry than any other Occidental beverage, but it lacks the full flavour of sherry, having a mild and not unpleasant flavour all its own. On the whole I rather liked *sake*, and I found myself able to detect the difference between ordinary *sake* and *sake* that was particularly good. While on this subject I may add that liquor of all sorts flows freely in Japan. *Sake* is the one alcoholic beverage generally served with meals in the Japanese style, but at the European-style luncheons and dinners I attended two or three kinds of wine were usually served, and there were cocktails before and sometimes liqueurs afterward. The Japanese have also taken up whisky-drinking to some extent. They import Scotch whisky and also make a bad imitation Scotch whisky of their own. But *sake* still reigns supreme as the national alcoholic drink, and when you see a Japanese intoxicated you may be pretty sure that *sake* — a lot of *sake* — did it.

From The China Lover *by Ian Buruma, 2008, a fictional first-person description of Yamaguchi Yoshiko's debut in Tokyo in 1940*
The Nichigeki gala concert was a triumph. The date was auspicious, for it fell on February 11, the 2600th anniversary day of our nation's foundation by Emperor Jinmu. Emperor Pu Yi had come to Tokyo especially for the occasion. Despite the cold weather, thousands of people lined up in front of the Imperial Palace to bow to our Emperor — and perhaps catch a glimpse of Emperor Pu Yi too, about whom there had been much written in the papers. Little did they know what I knew — that the Emperor of Manchukuo spent most of his time smoking opium and watching Charlie Chaplin movies. This was just one of the satisfactions of being in the information business. I knew things that ordinary people couldn't even imagine, not in a million years.

The scenes around the palace were nothing, however, compared to what was going on around the Nichigeki Theater. People had been out there all night, wrapped in overcoats and blankets, waiting for the box office to open. By nine o'clock in the morning there were three lines coiled round the building. By ten, it was five. And by the time the concert started at eleven, seven lines of people packed together in the freezing cold surrounded the theater. There was not an inch of room to move. The concert almost didn't begin at all, for Ri and her bodyguards couldn't get through the lines, which were like a solid wall of humanity. Policemen had to be called in to help the guards beat their way through with truncheons, and hustle poor Ri, who was hiding her face under the collar of her fur coat, into the stage door.

Yamaguchi Yoshiko (also known in East Asia as Ri Koran) was born in Manchuria in 1920 and became massively popular in both China and Japan. Ian Buruma's breathtaking The China Lover is a fictionalized look at her wildly improbable life, which ended in September 2014, when she was 94.

Crowds at Tokyo's Nichigeki Theater for Yamaguchi's 1940 performance

The Hidden Tokyo

From Tokyo *by Fosco Maraini, 1976*

I remember that I reached Tokyo for the first time on a bleak winter morning in 1938. The day was grey, the train I arrived on was grey, the city loomed grey beneath the overcast sky. The clothes in which the people of Tokyo scurried through the murk—even the kimono of which I had heard and expected so much, seemed dyed with a sodden, dull neutrality.

But I remember, too, that in that clay-coloured drabness the white gloves of the station masters and train attendants, the white seats on the multitude of rickshaws, the white slip covers inside the taxis had the visual shock of colour itself and seemed somehow to provide the finishing touch to a picture of smooth restrained professional composure.

Many years later I find myself still coming to grips with it. For each time I return to Tokyo I confront another city, one that is never quite like the Tokyo I knew on the preceding visit. New buildings spring up; attitudes change. Yet whenever I return I find lurking beneath the surface so much that is old, ageless. The real Tokyo, the hidden Tokyo, can be discovered only by someone with the time and patience to ferret it out.

Theater street in Asakusa in the 1930s

Delights for Young and Old

From A Strange Tale from East of the River *by Nagai Kafu, 1937*

Young and old delight in moving pictures and make them the subject of daily conversation, and even a person like me sometimes feels inclined to wonder what the conversation might be about. I always make it a special point, therefore, to look at billboards when I pass moving-picture houses. One can tell by the billboards, without seeing the pictures themselves, what the general plots are, and what delights people so.

A popular movie genre in the late 1920s: Edo-era outlaws

Lieutenant Yoshitada Niu, here speaking to his company on 26 February 1936, was executed for his leadership role in the Ni-Ni-Roku rebellion.

Government by Assassination

On 26 February 1936, more than 1,000 soldiers attempted a coup d'état in Tokyo, the most aggressive of many faction-based militaristic attacks on the government from the mid 1920s on. The coup leaders assassinated a number of government officials, including two former prime ministers, and occupied parts of downtown for days. Nineteen of the coup leaders were eventually executed, but the rebellion, commonly referred to as Ni-Ni-Roku ('26 February' in Japanese) became a major step towards the theological fascism to come. The Ni-Ni-Roku incident marked a climax in a years-long period dubbed 'government by assasination'.

Takahashi Korekiyo (here with his grandchild), former prime minister (13 November 1921 to 12 June 1922) and serving as finance minister at the time, was slashed and shot to death in his Akasaka home on 26 February 1936. Takahashi, sometimes called the 'Lord Keynes of Japan', was targeted in part because he'd had the audacity to promote a decrease in funding for the military. His house of the time has been shifted to the Edo-Tokyo Open Air Architectural Museum, in Tokyo's western suburb of Koganei. The bloodstains on the tatami have been cleansed.

147

One Thousand Stitches

From Earth and Soldiers, *by Hino Ashihei, 1938*
Speaking of the "thousand-stitches belt" reminds me of a recent episode that
may give you a clear insight into our minds and hearts, these days.

As you know, there is not a man aboard ship without one of these belts.
They encircle every waist and each stitch carries a prayer for safety. Mine is
of white silk and has a number of charms sewn into it. I do not understand
the symbolism connected with each. Some are Buddhist and others Shinto.
It makes no difference, of course. All are supposed to afford protection from
wounds.

Mother gave me an embroidered charm bag, which contains a talisman of
the "Eight Myriads of Deities," and a "Buddha from Three Thousand Worlds."

From Samurai! *by Sakai Saburo, 1957*
That evening I found several letters from home, and a small package from Fujiko. She had sent me a cotton band to wrap about my stomach, with one thousand red stitches; this was Japan's traditional talisman against enemy bullets.

Fujiko wrote, "Today we were told that our fatherland launched a great
war against the United States and Great Britain. We can only pray for our ultimate victory and for your good fortune in battle.

"Hatsuyo and I have stood at a street corner several hours a day for the last
several days, and have begged 998 women who passed to give us each a stitch
for this band. So it has the individual stitches of one thousand women. We
wish you will wear it on your body, and we pray that it may protect you from
the bullets of the enemy guns. . ."

Actually, few Japanese airmen held faith in the charm. But I knew what it
meant for Fujiko and my cousin to stand for long hours on the streets in the
cold air of winter. Of course I would wear it, and I wrapped it about my mid-
section.

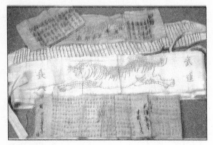

A thousand-stiches belt

*Women gather on a Ginza street corner to
stitch* senninbari, *'1,000 people's stiches' –
the goal was to get 1,000 women to each add a
stich to these belts.*

Let Us Refrain From Luxurious Dress!

From The Japanese Woman Looking Forward *by H. van Straelen, 1940*

It is really amazing and astonishing how the timid and humble Japanese woman, who for countless generations has quietly and modestly fulfilled her duty in the home, suddenly, with all her forces, is sharing the additional burden of her country. We see the happenings of things incredible, we thought, in Japan. For instance, since August 1, 1940, we see patrols of women on the streets of Tokyo handing out cards to all persons seen dressed luxuriously, calling their attention to the right recognition of the present situation of the country, the cards bearing such slogans as: "Let us refrain from luxurious dress," "Let us abolish rings." These public-spirited women are stationed at Hibiya, Yūrakucho, Ginza, Nihonbashi, Ueno, Shinjuku, Ikebukuro, all places well known, as crowded centers, to any visitor to Tokyo whether for only one week or more.

Nurses off to China from Tokyo Station, 1940

Above: *1940 signs warning Tokyoites about spies – roughly equivalent to 'loose lips sink ships'*

149

8 December 1941

In Japan, the Pearl Harbor attack happened on 8 December, not 7 December as it did in the United States, because of the international date line.

In Report From Tokyo *by Joseph Grew, 1942*
Almost immediately afterward the Embassy's gates were closed and locked by the police, and from that moment we were regarded and treated as prisoners. A group of Japanese radio experts then immediately came and went through all our houses with a fine-tooth comb, taking away all short-wave radio sets so that thereafter we should have no contact with the outside world save through the Japanese newspapers, which were regularly delivered to us.

Joseph Grew was the U.S. ambassador to Japan from 1932 until the war began. The Japanese military government quarantined him, along with all embassy staff from the U.S. and from other Allied nations, following the Pearl Harbor attack. He was released and returned to the United States in summer 1942.

Nagai Kafu's diary entry from 8 December 1941
Drafted first installment of novel *Ukimakura.* At dusk went as far as Doshubashi. Newspaper extras announcing war between Japan and the United States. Eating in a restaurant in Ginza on my way home when blackout announced and all street lamps and shop signs went out one after the other; but streetcars and automobiles kept their lights on. Scramble among passengers to get on streetcar for Roppongi; among them a patriot, who made a speech in a shrill voice.

The British ambassador and embassy staff in Tokyo in January 1942, under quarantine as of 8 December 1941, maintaining stiff upper lips.

The Spy Who Came In From … Germany

Richard Sorge, a German who spied for the Soviet Union, is widely recognized as one of the most accomplished spies of all time. His postings included London, various cities in Germany, Shanghai and finally Tokyo from 1933. He informed his Soviet handlers about Operation Barbarossa, Hitler's attack of the Soviet Union in June 1941, two weeks in advance (Stalin belittled the report), and then about Japan's subsequent disinclination to heed Hitler's pleas to invade Siberia – the Japanese were preparing to turn their attentions southward toward the resource-rich Dutch East Indies and were willing to attack the Soviet Union only when the latter was clearly on the ropes. This intelligence allowed the Soviets to concentrate their force westward, and is credited with having a critical influence on the outcome of the war.

Sorge was arrested in 1941 and hanged on 7 November 1944, in Tokyo's Sugamo Prison, in the Ikebukuro district of the city, the site four years later of the hangings of seven of the most notorious of Japan's convicted Class A war criminals.

From This Deception *by Hede Massing, 1951*

Physically, Sorge was a big man, tall and handsome, brown hair. His brow was creased and furrowed and his face lined. From a glance at his face you could tell that he had lived a hard and rough life. There was no arrogance or cruelty to the set of his eyes and the lines of his mouth.

He tipped off the Russians, and the United States, in turn, on the impending attack on Pearl Harbor sixty days before it happened. I believe him to be the only Russian agent who can be considered heroic by Americans.

He was executed by the Japanese. None of the newspaper accounts that appeared in this country did him justice. True, he was a spy. But he believed in what he did and he was a remarkable man, both proud and modest. And if he was ruthless—as some of the papers said—that, certainly, the Russians were responsible. He had started out a kind man and a good man.

. . . He did not fit the general pattern of the German Communist, neither did Christiane. They displayed better taste and more gusto than was customary in Communist circles. I liked them very much.

Sorge shortly before his execution

The wireless equipment discovered in Sorge's residence

Life During Wartime

From Made in Japan *by Morita Akio, 1986*

Everything the military-dominated government did was made to appear an order of the emperor, and they forced schoolchildren and adults alike to do incredible things. A school principal who made a mistake when he recited the Imperial Rescript on Education committed suicide to atone for it. Thought police and special police roamed the country arresting people on the slightest suspicion that they were not loyal or obedient enough or reverent enough. Conductors on the trolley cars that ran past the imperial palace grounds in Tokyo would announce the moment everybody was expected to bow. Schoolchildren bowed to the portable Shinto shrine that held the written words of the emperor. These were ways the military used to keep the nation in their power, and people like me and my parents went along. One might have dissent in his heart, and there were many who did, but it was difficult and dangerous to express it. Resisters were 'reeducated' in special camps, and those who still resisted were thrown into the most menial jobs. All leftists and Communists were rounded up and jailed.

The "Do-Nothing" Raid

On 18 April 1942, James Doolittle of the U.S. Air Force led a bombing raid on Tokyo and other locations on Japan's main island of Honshu – the first military attack on the Japanese home islands since the Black Ships. Wags in Tokyo rapidly rebranded Doolittle's raid the 'Do-Nothing' raid, because of its minimal impact on the Japanese economy and military power. Renaming notwithstanding, the raid, in which 16 B-25s dropped bombs on Tokyo and other cities in Japan, had a massive

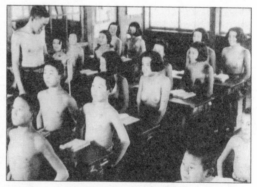

By 1941, so-called physical strengthening included co-educational nudity in the classroom.

effect on the mentality of the Japanese, and on wartime spirits in the USA. The raid had a much more lethal effect in mainland China: Japanese occupation forces there massacred hundreds of thousands in retaliation for the Chinese sheltering the raid's air crews after they (mostly) crash landed in eastern China.

From Daughter of the Pacific *by Matsuoka Yoko, 1952*
The Doolittle raid radically changed the casual attitude toward anti-air raid drills. The ladies were no longer shy about appearing in their *mompe*. Besides these ill-fitting trousers, we were asked to wear shoes instead of *geta* or *zori*, as Japanese footwear comes off too easily. Most women wore sneakers. A long-sleeved blouse, a pair of gloves, something to cover one's head, and a piece of white triangular cotton cloth (which would be needed in case of injury) completed the 'anti-air raid costume' . . .

Every Sunday morning around nine o'clock, the leader of the neighborhood Association, who served for a month in a system of rotation, would shout through his megaphone: "*Boku-enshu*! – Anti-air raid rehearsal!" From every house properly attired men and women would come out—each with an empty bucket—and line up in the middle of the street.

About this time, all unmarried girls who were not working outside of their homes were recruited to work in factories. It was no longer patriotic to marry young and bear many children. The old slogans disappeared from sight, and women were exhorted now to produce 'more airplanes.' Kyoko commented cynically, "It would take twenty years before a human being could be useful as a soldier. Apparently the Government decided they couldn't wait that long. And pregnant women are not very useful in factories."

Wartime fashion: mompe

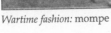

The Reluctant Admiral

Yamamoto Isoroku, reluctant architect of the Pearl Harbor attack, is apocryphally credited with 'I fear all we have done is wake a sleeping giant', the closing line of the 1970 movie Tora! Tora! Tora! *He studied at Harvard for two years, but his nuanced understanding of the United States went wasted in Japan's path toward war.*

Yamamoto was also famous for his high living. In the Tokyo geisha districts he frequented, he gained the nickname of "Eighty Sen," because the regular charge for a manicure was one yen, 80 sen was 80% of one yen, and Yamamoto's index and middle fingers on his left hand had been blown off when an enemy shell demolished a gun turret on the Imperial Japanese Navy's cruiser Nisshin during the Russo-Japanese War of 1904 – 1905.

Because the U.S. military had broken Japanese code by early 1942, they learned of Yamamoto's plan to fly to the Solomon Islands in April 1943, and shot him out of the sky during the attempt. He died instantly.

We land in America tomorrow. Many thanks for the cable you sent when we left. . . . I found it most unpleasant at Tokyo Station and Yokohama to have a lot of people from this or that league or association fussing around reading 'resolutions' and 'declarations'. It depresses and perturbs me to think that men like that pass as 'patriots'. . .

Letter from Yamamoto to a friend,
while he was en route to the London Naval Conference, 1934

From The Reluctant Admiral *by Agawa Hiroyuki, 1969 (tr 1979)*
Yamamoto's state funeral was held in Hibiya Park, in the center of Tokyo, on June 5, 1943 — the same day of the same month as the funeral of Admiral Togo Heihachiro nine years previously. The president of the funeral committee was Yonai Mitsumasa. The chief officiant was Shiozawa Koichi; both he and Yoshimasa, the chief mourner, wore Shinto-style robes and hats, and Yamamoto's widow Reiko wore formal dress of the kind worn by court ladies.

At 8 :50 that morning, members of the Musashi's *[Yamamoto's flagship]* crew carried Yamamoto's coffin, draped with a white cloth, from the room in which it had been lying in state in the Navy Club and placed it on a black gun carriage standing before the front entrance.

Led by a naval band playing Chopin's Funeral March, the procession descended the slope from the Navy Club, turned right, passing directly in front of Chiyoko's *[Yamamoto's primary mistress]* house in Kamiya-cho, then went

154

Yamamoto (second from left) at Tokyo Station, 1939

slowly on via the Toranomon crossing and the Uchisaiwai district. The people in the stand erected by the roadside for special acquaintances of the deceased were annoyed, they say, by press cameramen who, guessing that Chiyoko must be among them, tried to get a picture of her.

Turning the corner by the navy minister's official residence, the procession arrived at the site of the funeral ceremony in Hibiya Park at 9:50.

The altar and other structures customary at Japanese funerals were constructed simply of unvarnished wood with black-and-white striped curtains, a touch of color being provided by a bunch of roses sent by Mussolini. The military personnel present were commanded by General Doihara Kenji, and the approximately one thousand five hundred mourners included Prime Minister Tojo and many others whom Yamamoto himself would hardly have been delighted to see.

The opium addict and world-class war criminal Doihara joined Tojo as one of the seven men who had appointments with the gallows at Tokyo's Sugamo Prison on 23 December 1948. Agama's closing line here, 'hardly have been delighted to see', understates the case.

Turning Butter, and Boys and Girls, into Guns

From My Japan 1930 – 1951 *by Nakamoto Hiroko, 1970*

When the sirens sounded, we pulled on our *mompe*, the work slacks or coveralls we wore in the factory, and sat silent in the darkness, waiting for the all clear. Then we would tumble back into bed. But it seemed that before we could fall asleep, the sirens would start again and we would have to get up. The rules were that we had to be up when the sirens sounded and that we could not go back to bed until the all clear was heard. However, there were times when we were too tired to obey the rules. We did not care whether there were planes above us or not. All we children wanted was to sleep.

But there was no sleep.

I had my thirteenth birthday while working in the factory.

Wartime poster commemorating the founding of the Imperial Japanese Army. In vertical at the right is the slogan of one of myriad military PR campaigns, uchiteshi yamamu *('never stop fighting'), echoing Japan's earliest recorded literary work, the Kojiki, ironically itself an import – from China. Note the flags under the soldier's boot.*

From Report From Tokyo *by Joseph Grew, 1942*

Recently the Tokyo radio itself admitted that fourteen-year-old boys were being drafted as seamen. "Thus," it was announced, "the structure of victory will be prepared." The same radio has told how youngsters are being trained in the operation of tanks.

A 1940s rationing coupon for clothing

A private moment

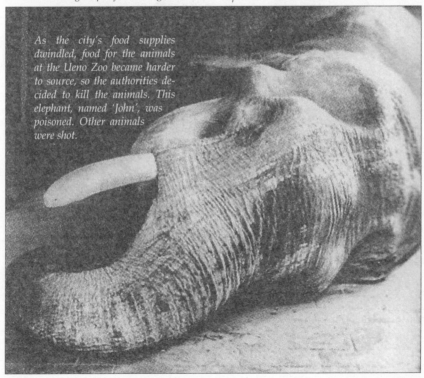

As the city's food supplies dwindled, food for the animals at the Ueno Zoo became harder to source, so the authorities decided to kill the animals. This elephant, named 'John', was poisoned. Other animals were shot.

Group bathing

A school shrine in Tokyo's Naka Meguro, 1942

Covers of Housewives' Magazine, Housewives' Friend *and* Housewives' Asahi, *1944*

With metals becoming increasingly scarce, these Ginza lightposts and traffic signs were torn down for recycling.

Divine Winds

The kamikaze *(meaning 'divine wind' in Japanese) of World War II, suicide pilots, were named for the typhoons that repelled the Mongol leader Kublai Khan's invading fleets from the Japanese coast in 1274 and 1281. Japanese opinion settled on the idea that the winds were divinely launched, contributing to the larger concept of the divinity of the emperor and, by extension, Japan itself. By 1944, many Japanese recognized that only divine intervention could prevent their utter defeat at the hands of the Allies, and some of their military leaders came up with the idea of what were essentially manned bombs, and hearkened back to a mythologized part of Japanese history for the name of these suicide bombers.*

With the official, euphemistic name Tokubetsu Kogetai, or Special Attack Forces, the kamikaze initiative began in October 1944, and with some initial perceived successes, the program expanded to its peak during the Battle of Okinawa (April – June 1945). Ultimately about 4,000 pilots (among them a dozen or so conscripted Koreans) perished, sinking about 50 Allied ships and damaging 300 more.

A graphic from the 1960 movie Aa – Tokubetsu Kogetai (Ah, the Special Attack Forces)

"Stop"

From **Samurai!** *by Saburo Sakai, Japan's second most successful fighter pilot to survive the war, with Martin Caidan and Fred Saito, 1957*
A *kamikaze* is a surprise attack, according to our ancient war tactics. Surprise attacks will be successful the first time, maybe two or three times. But what fool would continue the same attacks for ten months? Emperor Hirohito must have realized it. He should have said 'Stop.'

From A Tale for the Time Being *by Ruth Ozeki, 2013 – a fictional account of the mother of a soon-to-be kamikaze pilot in 1943*

"It was late October. There was a pagent. Twenty-five thousand student draftees marched into the compound outside Meiji Shrine. There were given rifles to carry on their shoulders like children playing soldiers. A cold, dull rain was falling, and the red and gold colors of the shrine looked gaudy and much too bright. For three hours the boys stood at attention, and we stood there too, listening to the fine words and phrases in praise of the fatherland.

The 'comfort bags' that soldiers were sent off to war with, containing a variety of things thought to be comforting to/protective of them.

"One of the boys, Haruki's classmate, gave a speech. 'We, of course, do not expect to return alive,' he said. They knew they would die. We had all heard of the mass suicides of soldiers at a place called Attu. Gyoukusai, *[suicide attack]* they called it. Insanity, but by then there was no stopping. The prime minister was there. Tojo Hideki. It is not true, what I said before, because I hated him. He was a war criminal, and after the war, they hanged him. I was so happy I wept for joy when I heard he was dead. Then I shaved my head and took a vow to stop hating.

Youths assembled for their send-off to war, in Tokyo's Meiji Jingu Gaien, 1943

A World Record

On the evening of 9 – 10 March 1945, the U.S. air forces, under the command of Major General Curtis LeMay, launched a firebombing attack that incinerated 100,000 or more citizens of Tokyo, an attack that beats Hiroshima for the gold medal in the category of largest anthropogenic death toll in a single day in human history. LeMay and his staff were so pleased with the technological achievement – creating conflagration via firebombs – that they continued the practice throughout the spring and early summer, focused on many of Japan's cities. Perhaps 250,000 people, mostly civilians, died as a result, in addition to the roughly 150,000 who died as a result of the atomic bomb attacks on Hiroshima and Nagasaki in August of the year.

From The Broader Way *by Mishima Sumie Seo, 1953*
In the eastern sky loomed a flight, another flight and yet another of B-29's. Keeping a 1,000 meter height and trailing white streamers of exhaust gas, they sailed in perfect formation through the blue-gold sky. To a purely aesthetic eye they looked like shawls of pearly fish riding through the seas of the universe . . . A pious American Japanese lady had once remarked that they looked exactly like angels, more like angels than any of the painted angels of the great masters...

So, completely apart from traditional religious associations, the ethereal beauty of the mighty bombers was Destiny itself to the people trembling below them.

From I Was Defeated *by Kodama Yoshio, 1959*
The majority of the dead were women. Some still had children strapped to their backs. Others had one child on their back and two dead children tucked beneath both arms. I saw with my own eyes the noble picture of the mother love of these women, who, despite the shower of incendiaries and the crashing detonation of ear-splitting bombs, had sought to protect the lives of their

young. All over the place I saw the burned corpses of mothers and children—floating like debris in ponds and on the sea, on scorched earth and on smoking piles of devastation. As I walked through the streets, I saw the smoke rising from numerous pyres of dead being cremated and smelt the stench of burning flesh. From the depths of my heart, I cried out against the cruelties of war and its sins.

Kodama wrote the manuscript for I Was Defeated *while locked up in Tokyo's Sugamo Prison after the end of the war, having been charged as a Class A war criminal, and having become one of the wealthiest people in Asia on proceeds from opium dealing and war profiteering. The U.S. CIA sprung him to conduct nominally anti-communist spywork in Asia, and he became one of the most notorious gangsters and 'kuromaku' ['black curtain' – éminence grise] of postwar Japan.*

Killing Japanese didn't bother me very much at the time . . . I suppose if I had lost the war, I would have been tried as a war criminal . . . every soldier thinks something of the moral aspects of what he is doing. But all war is immoral and if you let that bother you, you're not a good soldier.

Curtis LeMay, reflecting in later years

The Akasaka district with the Diet building in the background, spring 1945. Describing the firebombing, Mishima Yukio told a later audience: "it was the most beautiful fireworks display I have ever seen."

Colonel Kurtz opining in his last hours in 1979's Apocalypse Now
"They train young men to drop fire on people. But their commanders won't allow them to write 'fuck' on their airplanes because it's obscene!"

Neatly Piled–Up Rubble

From The China Lover *by Ian Buruma, 2008 – a fictionalized 1947 diary entry of the young occupation officer Donald Richie*

One day I was walking up the steps of Ueno Hill, the highest point in the flatlands bordering the Sumida River. You could see for miles around, a vista of neatly piled up rubble and cheap wooden houses with the occasional temple roof and stone lantern to show what had been there before that night in March 1945, when much of the city was laid to waste by our B-29s.

One of the survivors, right where I was standing, was the bronze statue of Takamori Saigo, the samurai rebel with the bulging eyes and thick eyebrows. He challenged the guns of the Westernized Meiji Army in a heroic and suicidal last stand in 1877. His samurai troops were armed with nothing but spears and swords. A hopeless enterprise, of course. According to legend (and who would wish to challenge that?), Saigo slit his own stomach in an honorable warrior's death. Japanese still regard their hero with immense affection and respect. He is remembered, among other things, for the extraordinary size of his balls.

So there he was on that cold and blustery day, Saigo of the big balls, standing watch like a sturdy peasant in the short kimono and straw sandals of his native region. At his feet was a swarm of homeless urchins, passing around cigarette butts, and eating whatever scraps of food they had managed to scrounge. The boys were dressed in shorts and tattered T-shirts, despite the cold. A few lucky ones had wooden sandals. And the truly fortunate ones found places to sleep in the warm corridors of the subway station at the bottom of the hill. I saw one little boy, who looked no older than five but might well have been more than ten, hold a rat by its tail, waving it in front of another child's face, to frighten him, or perhaps to show off what they were going to have for dinner that night.

An at-home bomb shelter in Nakano, west Tokyo. These were mostly worse than useless, in that they afford a false sense of security.

God only knows how these boys had survived the terrible night of the bombings. People who didn't melt or burn in the firestorm choked for lack of oxygen. Women tried to protect their faces from the "Flower Baskets," courtesy of General Curtis LeMay, by wrapping bundles of cloth around their heads. Many of them caught fire and ran around like human torches, their screams muffled by the roaring flames. Others tried to escape by jumping into the river, only to be boiled alive or catch fire as soon as they raised their heads above the scalding water.

All that remained of Ueno, or of Asakusa, a few miles farther north, were the concrete remnants of a few large department stores in a vast black hecatomb containing the charred bones of at least a hundred thousand people . . .

Survivors evacuating

Orphans being evacuated to safer areas in the countryside

The Emperor's Speech

On 14 August 1945, the Emperor recorded a 'surrender' speech to be broadcast the next day. The events surrounding the recording and subsequent broadcast on NHK became a combination of high drama and slapstick-worthy missteps. Die-hard (sic) militarists knew the recording had been made, and that it was still in the palace somewhere. They launched what is now known as the Kyujo Incident, occupying the palace, cutting phone lines, occasionally beating and killing along the way in their zeal to prevent the Emperor's recording from announcing the end of the war. When it became clear by mid morning on the 15th that they'd lost the struggle, that the recording had been spirited out of the palace (in a basket of soiled women's underwear that the militarists, also sexist, would recoil from searching), a few of the rebels killed themselves.

"We are about to broadcast something of the highest importance. All listeners please rise." Following this announcement on NHK just before noon on 15 August, the station played the national anthem, Kimigayo. "His majesty the Emperor will now read his Imperial Rescript for the Japanese people. We respectfully transmit his voice." In Hirohito: Behind the Myth *(1989), Edward Behr writes, "Hirohito listened, in the safety of his bunker. In the whole of Japan, he was probably the only able-bodied Japanese to do so sitting down."*

Bowing toward the palace after the speech

Listening to the emperor's speech

The Honorable Death of the Hundred Million

From Something Like an Autobiography *by Kurosawa Akira, 1982*

On August 15, 1945, I was summoned to the studio along with everyone else to listen to the momentous proclamation on the radio: the Emperor himself was to speak over the air waves. I will never forget the scenes I saw as I walked the streets that day. On the way from Soshigaya to the studios in Kinuta the shopping street looked fully prepared for the Honorable Death of the Hundred Million. The atmosphere was tense, panicked. There were even shopowners who had taken their Japanese swords from their sheaths and sat staring at the bare blades.

However, when I walked the same route back to my home after listening to the imperial proclamation, the scene was entirely different. The people on the shopping street were bustling about with cheerful faces as if preparing for a festival the next day. I don't know if this represents Japanese adaptability or Japanese imbecility. . . .

If the Emperor had not delivered his address urging the Japanese people to lay down their swords—if that speech had been a call instead for the Honorable Death of the Hundred Million— those people in that street in Soshigaya would have done as they were told and died. And probably I would have done likewise.

An unhappy child on a Tokyo department store roof in an earlier, happier day

167

Hirohito's Broadcast to the Nation, 15 August 1945

TO OUR GOOD AND LOYAL SUBJECTS:

After pondering deeply the general trends of the world and the actual conditions obtaining in Our Empire today, We have decided to effect a settlement of the present situation by resorting to an extraordinary measure.

We have ordered Our Government to communicate to the Governments of the United States, Great Britain, China and the Soviet Union that Our Empire accepts the provisions of their Joint Declaration.

To strive for the common prosperity and happiness of all nations as well as the security and well-being of Our subjects is the solemn obligation which has been handed down by Our Imperial Ancestors and which lies close to Our heart.

Indeed, We declared war on America and Britain out of Our sincere desire to ensure Japan's self-preservation and the stabilization of East Asia, it being far from Our thought either to infringe upon the sovereignty of other nations or to embark upon territorial aggrandizement.

But now the war has lasted for nearly four years. Despite the best that has been done by everyone - the gallant fighting of the military and naval forces, the diligence and assiduity of Our servants of the State, and the devoted service of Our one hundred million people - the war situation has developed not necessarily to Japan's advantage, while the general trends of the world have all turned against her interest.

Moreover, the enemy has begun to employ a new and most cruel bomb, the power of which to do damage is, indeed, incalculable, taking the toll of many innocent lives. Should We continue to fight, not only would it result in an ultimate collapse and obliteration of the Japanese nation, but also it would lead to the total extinction of human civilization.

Such being the case, how are We to save the millions of Our subjects, or to atone Ourselves before the hallowed spirits of Our Imperial Ancestors? This is the reason why We have ordered the acceptance of the provisions of the Joint Declaration of the Powers.

We cannot but express the deepest sense of regret to Our Allied nations of East Asia, who have consistently cooperated with the Empire towards the emancipation of East Asia.

The thought of those officers and men as well as others who have fallen in the fields of battle, those who died at their posts of duty, or those who met with untimely death and all their bereaved families, pains Our heart night and day.

The welfare of the wounded and the war-sufferers, and of those who have lost their homes and livelihood, are the objects of Our profound solicitude.

The hardships and sufferings to which Our nation is to be subjected hereafter will be certainly great. We are keenly aware of the inmost feelings of all of you, Our subjects. However, it is according to the dictates of time and fate that We have resolved to pave the way for a grand peace for all the generations to come by enduring the unendurable and suffering what is unsufferable.

Having been able to safeguard and maintain the structure of the Imperial State, We are always with you, Our good and loyal subjects, relying upon your sincerity and integrity.

Beware most strictly of any outbursts of emotion which may engender needless complications, or any fraternal contention and strike which may create confusion, lead you astray and cause you to lose the confidence of the world.

Let the entire nation continue as one family from generation to generation, ever firm in its faith in the imperishability of its sacred land, and mindful of its heavy burden of responsibility, and of the long road before it.

Unite your total strength, to be devoted to construction for the future. Cultivate the ways of rectitude, foster nobility of spirit, and work with resolution - so that you may enhance the innate glory of the Imperial State and keep pace with the progress of the world.

Commerce Among the Ruins

Urgent notice to enterprises, factories and those manufacturers in the process of shifting from wartime production to peacetime production. Your product will be bought in large quantities at a suitable price. Those who wish to sell should come with samples and estimates of production cost to the following address:
Shinjuku Market, 1-8-54, Tsunohazu,
Yodobashiku, Shinjuku, Tokyo

Kanto Ozu Gumi, 18 August 1945

From Tokyo Underworld – The Fast Times and Hard Life of an American Gangster in Japan, *by Robert Whiting, 1999*

It was surely some kind of record for speed. Three days after the end of the war—and a full ten before the first American soldier set foot in Japan—the above newspaper advertisement appeared for what would be the nation's first postwar black market. One of the very few paid announcements in print at the time, it was a call to commerce hardly anyone expected so quickly, given the wretched, bomb-ravaged condition of Tokyo.

Members of the Matsuda yakuza gang, which ran Tokyo's Shinbashi black market

Tokyo's Shinbashi black market, 1946

Okichis of the Showa Era

"Okichi" was the name of a concubine pro-
vided to Townsend Harris, first U.S. Consul
General to Japan (1856-1861). Okichi was
later mythologized as having sacrificed herself
nobly to salve the foreign barbarian's ap-
petites. The fascist term kokutai, *'national*
polity', was eventually suppressed by the oc-
cupation forces.

A dance organized for the U.S. military
troops at the Post Office Building in
Marunouchi by the RAA.

From Hirohito and the Making of Modern
Japan *by Herbert Bix, 2000*

On August 19 [1945] the Home Ministry ordered local government offices
to establish "Recreation and Amusement Associations" (RAA), funded from
the National Treasury. Almost overnight advertisements appeared in the
national press and elsewhere informing women in need that food, clothing,
and accommodation would be provided to all who volunteered to join. At the
inaugural declaration of the RAA, crowds formed on the Imperial Plaza and
an estimated fifteen hundred young women gathered on the street outside
the temporary headquarters of RAA at Ginza 7 chome *[in the vicinity of today's*
Matsuzaka Department Store]. There they listened as an RAA official read a
declaration stating:

"Through the sacrifice of thousands of Okichis of the Showa era, we shall
construct a dike to hold back the mad frenzy [of the occupation troops] and
cultivate and preserve the purity of our race long into the future . . . In this way
we shall contribute to the peace of society. Stated differently, we are volunteer-
ing [*our bodies*] for the preservation of the *kokutai*."

A few weeks after the emperor's radio broadcast, the first U.S. military forces to
enter Tokyo were greeted by an RAA delegation of prostitutes. Within a few more
weeks, the RAA had opened what some have suggested was the largest brothel in
the world at the time, the International Palace, in what is now the Tokyo suburb of
Funabashi. Japanese efficiency prevailed: occupation soldiers would remove their
shoes at the entrance and find them shined and waiting at the exit.

The boulevard that divides the downtown palace and its eastern moat from
Marunouchi, including MacArthur's headquarters in the Dai-Ichi Life building,
gained the nickname Hooker Alley. The moat had to be skimmed regularly, to re-
move the clogs of discarded condoms, because of the density of Japanese women in
the neighborhood who were renting themselves to the occupation troops.

171

The New Emperor's Pose

On 30 August 1945, General Douglas MacArthur landed at the nearby Atsugi airbase, beginning his six years as Supreme Commander of the Allied Powers (SCAP), based in Tokyo. He emerged from the plane and struck his well-rehearsed pose: casual, with hand in pocket, corncob pipe jutting from clenched jaws, sunglasses in place. MacArthur repeated the emergence ritual several times, to ensure that all photographers present could get a good shot.

MacArthur strides toward his waiting car at Atsugi, 30 August 1945 . His plane seen here, the Bataan, was named for the Bataan Death March in April 1942, in which thousands of Filipino and U.S. POWs died/were murdered. Famously declaiming 'I shall return', MacArthur retreated from the Philippines before the Japanese invasion and the subsequent March.

The famous picture of MacArthur and Hirohito, 27 September 1945, featuring MacArthur's carefully prepared informality.

The Dai-Ichi Life Insurance Building, commandeered for MacArthur's headquarters in September 1945, on the outer moat of the Imperial Palace. Wags subsequently nicknamed MacArthur the 'sotobori tenno' – 'the emperor at the outer moat' and the 'aome tenno' – 'the blue-eyed emperor'. The office is preserved and opens occasionally to the public.

172

Left: Tokyo Bay, 2 September 1945, when the surrender document was signed on board the USS Missouri. The U.S. military left no doubt as to who held power.

Demobbed troops returning to Tokyo. Around six million Japanese troops and civilians returned to Japan after the war.

A Dangerous, Destitute City

In a crime that would resonate decades later when Aum Shinrikyo murdered a dozen and sickened thousands on the Tokyo subways with a sarin gas attack in 1995, on 26 January 1948, a man wearing an armband identifying himself as a public health worker entered a branch of the Teikoku Ginko (Imperial Bank) in Shiinamachi, one stop from Ikebukuro on today's Seibu Ikebukuro line, just after closing time. Receiving the report of an outbreak of dysentery (a fairly common occurrence at the time) from 'armband man', and the directive that all bank staff should be inoculated, the bank manager had all staff assemble with their teacups.

'Armband man' then dropped 'medicine' into each cup, and directed all to drink it in unison upon his command. The 'medicine' he distributed was in fact poison. 16 people drank it, ten died within minutes, two others soon after. 'Armband man' scooped up about 160,000 yen, but for some reason left behind more than twice as much. He was never captured, though another man, Hirasawa Sadamichi, was wrongly held in prison for decades for the mass murder. He died there.

From The Broader Way *by Mishima Sumie Seo, 1953*
Nearly half the crowds were women—brown, wrinkled women, and chubby-cheeked little girls all hauling loads larger than themselves. And indeed, anyone having anything to carry on his back, felt sincerely happy, for countless burnt-out refugees, stripped of all earthly possessions, lay like discarded rags in the corners of the station hall.

The bodies lined up at the Teikoku Bank branch

Residential Tokyo, late 1945

The Shibuya station black market. To defend themselves against the heavily armed gangs and others, policemen and firemen were allowed to carry guns in the immediate postwar period in Tokyo.

Street scene in front of today's Ginza Wako building, then the Hattori Clock Tower, in 1946, when it served as a PX for the occupation forces.

The occupation force renamed Tokyo's Takarazuka theater 'Ernie Pyle', in honor of the beloved reporter who had been killed by a sniper during the Battle of Okinawa in April 1945. The theater reverted to its original name in 1955.

U.S. occupation troops on a day off at Yasukuni Shrine, 1946

Tokyo Skyline, 1947

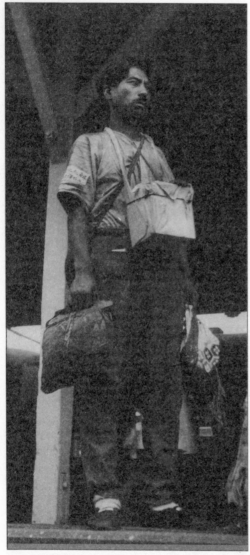

A returning soldier, with the remains of a comrade in the box on his chest.

An excerpt from Donald Richie's diary, published in Tokyo, *1999*

February 28, 1947, Winter – cold, crisp, clear – and Fuji stands sharp on the horizon, growing purple, then indigo in the fading light. I stand at the main crossing on the Ginza, nothing between me and the mountain. It is clear because there is no smoke, few factories, no fumes because the few cars are charcoal-burning. Fuji looks much as it must have for Hokusai and Hiroshige.

I stand and watch the mountain fade. From this crossing it had not been seen since Edo times; but now all the buildings in between are cinders. Between me and Fuji is a burned waste-land, a vast and blackened plain where a city had once stood.

At this crossing there are only two large buildings standing. The Ginza branch of the Mitsukoshi Department Store, gutted, hit by a fire-bomb, even the window frames twisted by the heat. Across the street is the other, the white stone Hattori Building with its clock tower: much as it had been with its cornices and pediments.

There is not much else left: the ruins of the burned-out Ka-buki-za, the round, red, drum-like Nichigeki, undamaged. At Yurakucho, on the edge of the Ginza, are a few office buildings and the Tokyo Takarazuka Theatre, now renamed the Ernie Pyle, and the Hibiya and Yurakuza motion-picture theatres.

Otherwise block after block of rubble, stretching to the horizon. Wooden buildings did not survive the fire storms of the American bombers. Those that stood were made of stone or brick. Yet, already, among these there is the yellow sheen of new wood. People are returning to the city.

I see them shuffling along the pavements, all those now returning. One somehow expects festivity – there were so many people shambling along or lounging about. But there are no laughter and little conversation. And it is dark, this Ginza which had once been a fountain of light. Now it is lit only by the passing headlights of Occupation jeeps and trucks, and the acetylene torches in the night stalls.

Here everything is being sold - the products of a vanished civilization. There were wartime medals and egret feather tiaras and top hats and beaded handbags. There were bridles and bits and damascene cufflinks. There were ancient brocades and pieces of calligraphy, battered woodblock prints and old framed photographs. Everything is for sale - or for barter.

Stopping, looking, handling, passing, were the people. Uniforms are still everywhere - black student uniforms, army uniforms, young men wearing their forage caps, or their army boots, or their winter-issue overcoats; others were in padded kimono, draped with scarves; women still in kimono or those *mompe* trousers used for farm work which in the cities had served as wartime dress. And many wear face-masks because of winter colds. Also, everyone was out of fashion: in peacetime they are still dressed for war.

How quiet the crowd is. The only sounds are the scufflings of boots, shoes, wooden sandals. These and the noises of the merchandise being picked up, turned over, put down. The merchants make no attempt to sell. They sit and look, smoking a pinch of tobacco in long-stemmed brass pipes, staring at the black throng passing in the darkness of an early evening.

I look at faces: an old woman illuminated by a passing truck, the white profile of a young student in the acetylene glare, a mother, the blank round faces of her two children. Well over a year had passed since the unthinkable occurred and the unendurable endured. I was regarding a populace still in shock. There was an uncomprehending look in the eyes. It was a look one sometimes still sees in the eyes of children or the very ill.

And in the eyes of convalescents as well. Shacks are being built, any which way, new streets are formed, a hut here, a shack there. Yet Tokyo is a city of the dead. So many were killed, so many were burned or boiled in the firebomb raids. The survivors remembered.

Demokurashii

Thousands of labor unions and other formerly banned associations appeared or reappeared post-war in a new democratic era. A founder and former chair of Sony, Morita Akio, describes the era as 'a heady time for the long-suppressed liberals, socialists and Communists'. Tokyo's May Day parade of 1946 became a riot of protestors, some trying to breach the walls of the Imperial Palace.

From The Hidden Sun *by Dorothy Robins-Mowry, 1983*
[The reporter] stopped a tiny, bent old lady in dark *kimono* and somber *obi*. "Did you vote?" he asked. "*Mochiron* — of course," she answered. "How did you vote?" "It is a secret ballot," she replied and peered up at him with bright shrewd eyes, glad, I am sure, to give back the information that the nation's radio for two or three months had been dinning into her ears from 6 a.m. to 12 p.m.

I laughed. He laughed and patted her on the back. "You're all right," he said. "But tell me this. How did you make your decision?" His interpreter went off into paragraphs of explanation during which I caught the words 'husband' and 'eldest son' and I knew that he was asking the old lady who had told her how to vote.

She appreciated the point and paused a moment as if to savor it. "Well," she finally said, "I listened to my husband. I listened to my eldest son. I listened to the ward officials. I went to the meetings and I listened. And then I thought it all over and voted the way I thought was best. It is a secret ballot!" That disposed of the matter.

The lead banner says 'Protect Working Mothers'.

Election posters in Ginza, 1946

Women first gained the right to vote in 1946.

First female leaders in the Diet appear in a press conference – with English titles conveniently provided for foreign reporters.

LEFT: *A novel topic for a publication from the Ministry of Education, 1946* **RIGHT:** *"Renouncing war", a now-famous graphic in* Story of the New Constitution, *published by the Ministry of Education in 1947*

179

The Tokyo Trials

From Windows for the Crown Prince *by Elizabeth Grey Vining, 1953*

Ever since I had been in Tokyo the International Military Tribunal of the Far East, familiarly known as the War Crimes Tribunal, had been sitting. Eleven judges representing the eleven allies in the war against Japan sat on the bench facing twenty-five Japanese defendants, who had been indicted on charges of conspiring to wage aggressive war in violation of international law and treaties, and of abstaining from taking adequate steps to prevent breaches of the laws and customs of war: in other words, of responsibility for the atrocities and horrors of the prisons and internment camps.

Tojo Hideki in the dock at the Trials.

When the prosecution was presenting its case, in 1946 and early 1947, the Japanese newspapers carried, by order of the Occupation, full reports of the excesses and outrages committed by the Japanese Army and Navy, and the Japanese people read them, shocked and sickened by the things which they learned for the first time had been done in their name. There is no doubt that these things were done, and all who have come to love and respect the Japanese people must accept the fact which they find difficult to explain: that people so self-controlled, courteous, and kindly in their daily dealings with others could be in warfare so arrogant and so cruel. The explanation lies in the words *in warfare*. War makes beasts of us all. The American people still are in happy ignorance of atrocities committed by our own men in the Pacific. Whether there were many, I do not know. I have heard only whispers, and a single instance, told to me by a captain in the United States Navy, which I wish I could erase from my memory.

Facing [*the prosecution*] in two rows were the defendants. The general effect was that of a collection of tired, bored, seedy, discredited men. It seemed almost incredible that they could have had any connection with the might and fury and horror of aggressive war.

> "What are the feelings of the Emperor? He cannot continue to conceal his responsibility for war crimes."
>
> Kokusai Times, 1946

Shielding the Emperor

Telegram from MacArthur to then General Dwight Eishenhower, quoted from Hirohito and the Making of Modern Japan *by Herbert Bix, 2000*

[*Hirohito's*] indictment will unquestionably cause a tremendous convulsion among the Japanese people, the repercussions of which cannot be overestimated. He is a symbol which unites all Japanese. Destroy him and the nation will disintegrate. . . it is possible that a million troops would be required which would have to be maintained for an indefinite number of years.

Bix asserts: "No official U.S. document unearthed so far has indicated that MacArthur or his staff investigated the emperor for war crimes. What they investigated were ways to protect Hirohito from the war crimes trials."

Hirohito portrayed on a sea of skulls in Shinso, *a satirical magazine, in 1950.*

Sugamo Prison in 1948. It was razed in the 1970s to make way for the Sunshine 60 building, in Ikebukuro, Japan's tallest building for nearly 20 years.

The Message on Tojo's Teeth

Rookie Navy dentist Jack Mallory, then 22, was assigned to craft dentures for Tojo Hideki, former prime minister and general in the Imperial Japanese Army, in late 1946, while Tojo was imprisoned at Tokyo's Sugamo prison. Military practice was to engrave a soldier's name, rank and serial number on dentures – Mallory gave the practice a novel twist: Prompted by colleague George Foster and others, he engraved, in Morse code, 'Remember Pearl Harbor' on Tojo's dentures. Word of the prank leaked in early 1947, at which time Mallory's commanding officer said, "That's funny as hell, but we could get our asses kicked for it," and Mallory returned to Sugamo to borrow Tojo's new dentures and grind down the Morse dots and dashes.

Just before he left Japan, Mallory attended the Tokyo Trials (April 1946 – November 1948) in the former Imperial Japanese Army headquarters in the Ichigaya district of Tokyo. Tojo recognized him at the hearings, pointed at the dentures, and bowed. Tojo had earlier said that dentures didn't matter so much, as he probably wouldn't be needing them for long. He was right – he was hung in Sugamo on 23 December 1948 along with six other convicted Class A war criminals.

The story of Mallory's dental diversion became widely publicized only in the 1990s. Mallory was quoted at the time: "It's just not that many people that had a chance to get those words into his mouth."

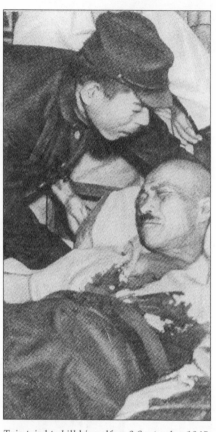

Tojo tried to kill himself on 8 September 1945, as occupation forces were closing in, with a pistol shot to the torso. He missed his heart, despite the target having been drawn on him by a doctor. On being arrested, he said, "I am very sorry it is taking me so long to die. The Greater East Asia War was justified and righteous. I am very sorry for the nation and all the races of the Greater Asiatic powers. I wait for the righteous judgment of history. I wished to commit suicide but sometimes that fails."

What Does Makudonarudo Mean?

The Japanese have been importing words and language for at least 1,500 years, when they imported an entire writing system, the Chinese characters, which became their first. (The Japanese themselves are imports to the Japanese archipelago – their ancient ancestry hails from what is now Korea and China and S.E. Asia.) As their encounters with the West increased starting about 1500 CE, they began importing Western words – the current Japanese word for bread, pan, traces back to Japan's early encounters with the Portuguese, 500 years ago, while their word for a part-time or short-term job, arubaito, comes from the German arbeit, work.

Because the Japanese language supports only a very few double consonant pronunciations, and no consonantal word endings save the 'n' sound (and the 's' sound in informal speech), the importation of foreign words (gairaigo – literally 'language from outside') can create challenges. For example, the German arbeit gets Japanized by putting a 'u' between the 'r' and the 'b', and by putting a vowel at the end. Thus, a two-syllable word in German becomes a four-syllable word in Japanese – アルバイト, arubaito.

Makudonarudo is the Japanese pronunciation of a famous Western brand hugely popular in Japan – a word Japanese teachers love to tease their foreign beginning students about, because it so little represents the English word: McDonalds!

New Design, one of the first post-war publications to revisit fashion, which had been largely proscribed in the war years

'Living art' became hugely popular postwar, for rather obvious reasons. This model poses as Reubens' Andromeda.

Young Editors

Sato Hideo recalls momentous changes in his school experience after the war ended, related in Japan at War *by Teruko and Theodore Cook, 1992*

I was born in war. It was always around. But war is fun. Boys like war.

At the end of my sixth-grade year, we painted out the passages in our textbooks which the American occupiers considered offensive. Up to then, textbooks had been something you felt fortunate to have. You bowed to them before you opened them. Now we cut out pages and blackened out whole passages with ink.

An example of the handiwork of Sato and his classmates

Street card game, late 1940s

The Prince and I

"If anything I have ever done has been a success, it was asking Mrs. Vining to come here."
Hirohito gloating on Elizabeth Grey Vining's tutelage of his son, Akihito, after the tutelage had proven a success. She was born in Philadelphia and died in 1999 at the age of 97.

Another Future Leader

Sony's 1947 rice cooker was the first step in their transition from a radio repairing company. It wasn't very successful ...

Then crown prince Akihito and his tutor, Elizabeth Grey Vining, 1947

... but other initiatives proved more promising – this is their first tape recorder, 1950 ...

... and the first transistor radio, 1955.

A company photo at Sony, 1951

Zaibatsu

These conglomerates (zaibatsu may be translated as 'financial clique') held powerful sway over the Japanese economy from the late 19th century through the end of the war. Some of MacArthur's occupation leaders, intellectual children of FDR's New Deal, strove to break them up, but the Cold War and the purpoted goal of defeating Communism defeated those efforts. The Big Four zaibatsu: Mitsubishi, Mitsui, Sumitomo, Yasuda. The descendants of the zaibatsu are today's keiretsu (economic groups).

Today's top keiretsu include Mitsubishi, Mitsui and Sumitomo. Yoko Ono is a descendant of the Yasuda family, and a survivor of the March 1945 firebombing of Tokyo – her family had a secure shelter in the then western suburb of Azabu.

Kasutori Culture

From *Villon's Wife* by Dazai Osamu, 1947

"Mrs. Otani, my wife and I run a little restaurant near the Nakano Station. We both originally came from the country, but I got fed up dealing with penny-pinching farmers, and came to Tokyo with my wife. After the usual hardships and breaks, we managed to save up a little and, along about 1936, opened a cheap little restaurant catering to customers with at most a yen or two to spend at a time on entertainment. By not going in for luxuries and working like slaves, we managed to lay in quite a stock of whisky and gin. When liquor got short and plenty of other drinking establishments went out of business, we were able to keep going.

"The war with America and England broke out, but even after the bombings got pretty severe, we didn't want to be evacuated to the country, not having any children to tie us down. We figured that we might as well stick to our business until the place got burnt down. Your husband first started coming to our place in the spring of 1944, as I recall. We were not yet losing the war, or if we were we didn't know how things actually stood, and we thought that if we could just hold out for another two or three years we could somehow get peace on terms of equality. When Mr. Otani first appeared in our shop, he was not alone. It's a little embarrassing to tell you about it, but I might as well come out with the whole story and not keep anything from you. Your husband sneaked in by the kitchen door along with an older woman. I forgot to say that about that time the front door of our place was shut, and only a few regular customers got in by the back."

A bar serving kasutori, Tokyo's postwar equivalent of 'moonshine' or 'bathtub gin'

Dazai, pen-name of Tsushima Shuji, was one of Tokyo's most prominent chroniclers of the postwar kasutori *culture, and one of its most devoted acolytes. After a half-dozen previous suicide attempts, the first during his high school years, he managed to die by drowning himself with his paramour in west Tokyo's Tamagawa River in 1948.*

The Most that Can Be Expected

From Development of the Japanese Society since VJ Day, *12 March 1947 Candidate for top-ten misapprehensions of the 20th century . . .*

Japan will be faced with most serious obstacles in her efforts to revert to her former industrial structure, partly because raw silk has lost its former preeminent position in international trade, and partly because of the fear of Japanese competition on the part of Western industries. The most that can be expected is a 'modest' participation in international trade, and, by the same token, a small degree of industrial rehabilitation.

Police dismantling a kasutori *still, 1946*

Tokyo Tower, built in part from scrap from tanks destroyed in the Korean War, opens in 1958. The Korean War proved an astounding boon for the recovering Japanese economy starting in 1950, as the United States needed a close-by staging area and industrial base to prosecute the war happening a half hour's flight west of Japan's westernmost main island, Kyushu.

One of many demobbed soldiers who were forced to hustle for sustenance post-war

Coming and Going…

From Windows for the Crown Prince *by Elizabeth Grey Vining, 1952*
Transportation was hideous. Trains and street-cars were cold, dirty, and often windowless as well as jammed to the roof. People climbed in through the windows after the aisles and steps were filled. Cloth of all kinds was so scarce that even the worn green plush upholstery had been cut off by passengers and taken home to patch clothes. It was not unusual for people to have their ribs broken in the crush, and I myself saw a pencil that had been splintered in a man's breast pocket. One of my pupils wrote, "My foot are stepped on, my hair are drew, my hands are caught. I feel like canned sardine."

Most of my pupils spent from two to five hours a day in these trains.

From Tokyo Year Zero *by David Peace, 2007*
This is the New Japan; Mitaka station swarming with hundreds, thousands of people waiting for trains in both directions; to travel out into the countryside to sell their possessions off cheap to buy food; to travel into Tokyo to sell food to buy other people's possessions cheap, endlessly back and forth, forth and back, endlessly buying and selling; selling and buying; the New Japan –

Immediately post-war, Tokyoites were desperate to visit the rural areas, where food and other necessities were more easily found.

From Thousand Cranes *by Kawabata Yasunari, 1949-1952*

As the train approached Tokyo Central Station, he looked down upon a tree-lined avenue. It ran east and west, almost at right angles to the railroad. The western sun poured into it, and the street glittered like a sheet of metal. The trees, with the sun behind them, were darkened almost to black. The shadows were cool, the branches wide, the leaves thick. Solid Occidental buildings lined the street.

There were strangely few people. The street was quiet and empty all the way to the Palace moat. The dazzlingly bright streetcars too were quiet. Looking down from the crowded train, he felt that the avenue alone floated in this strange time of evening, that it had been dropped here from some foreign country.

In 1946 and 1947, Kodaira Yoshio, one of the soldiers who had returned from the Japanese rape and pillage of China, continued by raping and murdering about ten women in Tokyo and Tochigi Prefecture. Peace's Tokyo Year Zero *is an astonishingly great fictionalization of the case.*

Unfortunate development at Tokyo's Mitaka Station, 1949 . . .

. . . and one in Nishi Nippori in 1962 – this one killed 160 people

189

Sayonara to SCAP, Hello to Consumption

In April 1951, U.S. President Truman famously relieved MacArthur of his role as Commander in Chief of the U.N. forces in Korea, and Supreme Commander for the Allied Powers (SCAP) in Japan, for insubordination. MacArthur, a consummate showman, had his staff work with the Japanese authorities to ensure a suitable departure, which included hundreds of thousands of Japanese waving little U.S. flags on the general's route from SCAP HQ. In addition, the national radio channel, NHK, played what remains a message indicating 'time to go home' in Japanese public establishments to this day: Auld Lang Syne. Students were dismissed from school, and Prime Minister Yoshida waved goodbye as the same plane that had brought MacArthur to Tokyo six years earlier lifted off from Tokyo's Haneda Airport.

MacArthur waves goodbye to the crowd.

From MacArthur's address to the U.S. Congress on 19 April 1951, his last official appearance.

The Japanese people since the war have undergone the greatest reformation recorded in modern history. With a commendable will, eagerness to learn, and marked capacity to understand, they have from the ashes left in war's wake erected in Japan an edifice dedicated to the supremacy of individual liberty and personal dignity, and in the ensuing process there has been created a truly representative government committed to the advance of political morality, freedom of economic enterprise, and social justice.

The launch of the Rabbit scooter, 1953

The famous Japanese love for photography revives post-war.

First broadcast of the Kohaku, still the national New Year's Eve program, in 1951

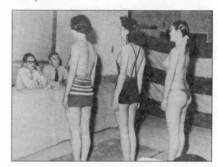

Would-be strippers auditioning in Yurakucho's Nichigeki, 1951

Tokyo Rose

This was the name given to roughly a dozen women who served as on-air personalities representing the Japanese theological dictatorship during the war years, broadcasting English-language programs aimed at demoralizing Allied troops. Iva Toguri D'Aquino (right) became the symbol of the Tokyo Rose phenomenon – she was arrested in September 1945 and imprisoned in both Japan and the United States despite a lack of evidence of crime.

Fascists, Version 3.0 …

Captured in Nagao Yasushi's Pulitzer-winning photograph, Yamaguchi Otoya has just withdrawn the blade from the abdomen of the head of the Japan Socialist Party, Asanuma Inejiro, in Tokyo's Hibiya Hall on 12 October 1960. The 17-year-old Yamaguchi hung himself in his jail cell a few weeks later, after writing 'seven lives for my country – long live the emperor' on the wall with a toothpaste/water combination. 'Seven lives for my country' was a hat tip to the last words of a famous samurai of the 1300s.

Yamaguchi's picture in the center of an altar at a hall belonging to the "Great Japan Patriot's Party". The Meiji emperor (top right) joins Yamaguchi, in, er, surprising company.

…and Those They Revered …

Then crown prince Akihito marries commoner Shoda Michiko, 10 April 1959 (above). The city celebrated with, among other things, flower-bedecked trollies (facing page, upper right) and a giant Japanese flag image on Ginza's Matsuya department store (below).

Why My Life May Be Shortened

From My Life Between Japan and America *by Edwin O. Reischauer, 1986*

. . . the reason why my life may be shortened is not overwork in Tokyo but because of an entirely unpredictable incident that happened on March 24, 1964.

Exactly at noon that day I started to leave the Chancery for a luncheon engagement with Kiom Chong P'il, the outsted Korean military leader. Normally the Marine guard would jump up from his desk and salute me at the door of the Chancery, but he happened to be on the phone. As I was passing through the doorway, I bumped into a small, slightly built Japanese in a seedy-looking raincoat who seemed decidedly out of place in the Embassy. I turned to the people in the lobby and said something like "Where is this man going?" He looked up at me, his face lit up, and he lunged at me with a long kitchen knife. Because we were so close and he so small, he did not have time to raise the knife — if he had this book would never have been written — but plunged it straight into my right thigh, where the tip broke off against my thigh bone. Luckily the bone protected my main nerve, saving me from being a cripple for the rest of my life.

U.S. ambassador Edwin Reischauer recovers in a Tokyo hospital, wife Haru at his side, after the assassination attempt.

Work Hard, Play Hard, Drink Hard

From City Life in Japan *by Ronald Dore, 1958*

'Work hard, play hard, drink hard, and make up for loss of sleep with Benzedrine and vitamin injections' seems to be the admired regimen of many middle-class Tokyo Japanese men, particularly those who would count themselves as intellectuals. Ruth Benedict remarks on the Japanese belief in the superiority of spirit over matter and notes that they lack the American's tendency to consider the body as a machine from which one can only get out the equivalent of the energy one puts in. But the Japanese are not lacking in this notion; rather the difference lies in their attitudes toward machines. If the American treats them with respect and considers their requirements absolute, the Japanese treats them with familiar contempt, expects them to run with the minimum of maintenance in crises, and places great reliance on emergency patching-up.

Tokyo's Korakuen amusement park opened in 1955.

A City of Firsts, . . .

From Belli Looks at Life and Law in Japan *by Melvin Belli, 1960*

Tokyo is not a city with towering skyscrapers. Its buildings must be constructed according to certain strict regulations of height, as has been the law until recently in occasionally earthquaked Los Angeles. Since Tokyo is famous for its many earthquakes, its buildings sprawl over many acres instead of reaching into the sky as in New York and Chicago.

Tokyo today has some of the largest *firsts*. Besides being the largest city in the world, Tokyo, and Japan, is first in movie making, first in shipbuilding, and cer-

1962 ad for the newly launched vitamin and stimulant drink, Lipovitan D.

tainly first in the resurgence and fervor of economic endeavor. Everyone pedals a little harder on his bicycle in Japan than in other countries, everyone works a little longer. It is not unusual to have a daytime job as well as a night-time job. The vibrant force in the Orient today is Japan. Tokyo is cosmopolitan. It has a spatter of France, Russia, Germany, Italy and, certainly, of America in its culture, in its cooking, its dress, its manufacture, its transportation, its airplanes, its pleasures and games as well as its laws.

...and a Full City

From Japanese Blue Collar *by Robert E. Cole, 1971*

Housing is a chronic problem, particularly for urban blue-collar workers. Many of them live in small, one-room apartments. In Tokyo, for example, where one out of every ten Japanese lives, 29 percent of the households faced "housing difficulties" in 1963 according to a government agency. Households were classified as facing difficulties if they were confined to less space per person than 2.5 mats (45 square feet), if they were housed together with another household, or if they were housed in buildings other than dwellings. When these households are added to those defined by the agency as "exceedingly cramped," they total 757,000; this means that 35 percent of all the families in Tokyo are inadequately housed.

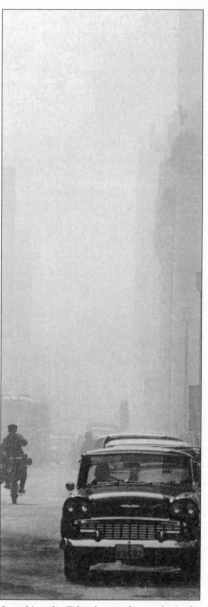

Something else Tokyo became famous for in the 1960s – smog

The Other Emperor

Outside Japan, Kurosawa Akira is easily the country's most famous filmmaker, and
Seven Samurai *perhaps his most famous work. His nickname at Tokyo's Toho Studios, his professional home for most of his 30 films, was* Tenno – The Emperor – *because of his domineering approach to direction. The American classic* The Magnificent Seven *was an acknowledged homage to Kurosawa's* Samurai.

From Cannon Fodder – What it means to call Seven Samurai a great film. *Article by Chris Fujiwara in the Boston Phoenix, August 2002*
In a 2002 poll of international directors and critics, 12 directors and 15 critics named Kurosawa's 1954 Seven Samurai as one of the 10 best films of all time. On the directors' poll, it tied for ninth place. . . . On the Internet Movie Database, Seven Samurai now ranks eighth (tied with Star Wars) among the top 250 movies as chosen by the site's registered users.

Shimura Takeshi, who acted for Kurosawa in 20 of the director's films, as the lead samurai in Seven Samurai.

196

Shimura (far left), Mifune Toshiro (second from right) and other members of Kurosawa's 'gumi', his stable of actors with whom he worked constantly, in their Seven Samurai roles.

From The Films of Akira Kurosawa *by Donald Richie, 1965 – "written by Minoru Chiaki upon being asked for a word-portrait of Akira Kurosawa"*

A fishing spot along [Tokyo's] Tamagawa River.
Kurosawa and Chiaki are fishing.
It is during the shooting of Seven Samurai: only half the film is finished, the budget is all used up, shooting is interrupted.

Chiaki: *So what's going to happen?*

Kurosawa: *Well, the company isn't going to throw away all the money it's already put into the film. So long as my pictures are hits I can afford to be unreasonable. Of course, if they start losing money then I've made some enemies.*

Money is found, shooting is begun again; money is used up, shooting is interrupted. Kurosawa and Chiaki go fishing again.

Kurosawa: *(Dangling his line with some satisfaction.) Now that they've gotten in this deep, they have no choice but to finish it!*

Chiaki Minoru (second from left above) was one of Kurosawa's favorite actors, appearing in seven of the director's films.

Mifune Toshiro as the lead in Rashomon. *Mifune acted in 16 of Kurosawa's films, famously parting company with the director following the shooting of* Red Beard, *because Mifune's requirement to grow and keep the beard prevented him from gaining other work.*

Godzilla *also debuted in 1954 – the Japanese name, Gojira, is a mashup of the Japanese for gorilla (gorira) and whale (kujira).*

Another Enduring Japanese Contribution

From Ways of Forgetting, Ways of Remembering *by John W. Dower, 2012*

A campaign to ban all nuclear weapons, initiated by Japanese housewives in May 1954, for example, soon collected an astonishing 30 million signatures. This same turbulent period also saw the birth, in November 1954, of Godzilla, Japan's enduring contribution to the cinematic world of mutant science-fiction monstors spawned by a nuclear explosion.

Another screen icon, Atomu, known as Astro Boy in the West, debuted in 1952.

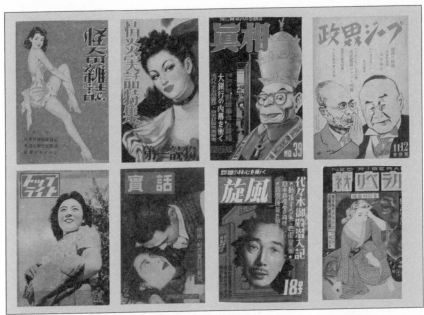

A sample of the spate of postwar publications

The cast in one of the first postwar radio variety shows

Foreigners Making It Big

Legally Japanese, But...

Kim Sin-rak, born in a province of what is now North Korea, debuted as a sumo wrestler in 1940, taking the ring name Rikidozan and eventually becoming a sekiwake, the third-highest rank in the sport. He began his next career, as a 'professional wrestler' in 1951, and became an icon in Japan with his (scripted of course) defeats of much larger Western opponents, providing some salve for Japanese psyches injured by the utter defeat in the war and subsequent occupation. Rikidozan's wrestling performances were among the first television programming in the country and contributed massively to increases in TV sales. Infirm viewers sometimes died from heart attacks when Rikidozan's performances took unexpected turns.

His handlers worked hard to conceal Rikidozan's Korean ancestry, as his multi-millionaire status as defender of Japanese pride would have been destroyed had the Japanese publicly recognized what many privately knew. Rikidozan aligned closely with Tokyo's Korean-dominated Tosei-kai mob. He was stabbed with a urine-soaked blade in the equally infamous New Latin Quarter Club in 1963, by a member of the rival, ethnic Japanese-dominated Sumiyoshi-kai mob. He died ten days later of peritonitis, amid suspicion that his murder had been directed by the U.S. CIA.

Technically, Rikidozan wasn't a foreigner. As he was born on the Korean Peninsula in 1924, which had been annexed by Japan in 1910, he was legally a Japanese citizen from birth. But that mattered nothing practically.

Rikidozan performs his signature karate-chop move in a performance with Killer Kowalski.

Rikidozan's wedding in 1963 to a police inspector's daughter, ironic given his deep ties to organized crime, preceded his death by six months.

Zappetti in 1983, upon being granted Japanese citizenship and taking the family name Koizumi, oddly the same family name that Lafcaido Hearn had taken upon his own assumption of Japanese citizenship 80 years earlier.

The Mafia Boss of Tokyo

In 1956, after many years of black-market dealing and one jail stint for a famously botched jewel heist, Nick Zappetti founded Tokyo's first pizzeria, Nicola's, which helped establish Roppongi as a noir entertainment destination in the years leading up to the Olympics.

Zappetti was widely referred to as The Mafia Boss of Tokyo, a moniker he didn't mind at all.

ABOVE: The New Otani in 1964, the latest in a series of pre-Olympic new hotel construction – the Palace in 1961, the Okura in 1962, the Tokyo Hilton in 1963. The New Otani served as a primary location in 1967's You Only Live Twice, the fifth in the James Bond/007 movies of the era.

One Vision of Tokyo . . .

From Windows for the Crown Prince *by Elizabeth Grey Vining, 1952*

The old street cries of Tokyo were coming back, and with them a little of the normal life and color of the past. When I first came to Japan, the only street cry was that of the man who went about at night clapping two sticks together and calling out his long-drawn warning, "*Hi-no-yo-jin*! Be careful of fires." Spring had brought the goldfish man, summer the wind-bell man, who needed no cry, for all the fairy bells on his cart tinkled and delicately clashed as he moved along the uneven road. With the autumn came the bamboo-seller's nasal whine, as he pulled a two-wheeled cart piled with long green bamboo poles, the wail of the mender of bat-umbrellas— "*Ko-mo-ri-ga-sa!*"—the shriller cry of the tinman who would repair pots and pans. In the crisp early mornings came the call of the little boy who sold fermented beans wrapped in straw, a breakfast delicacy; "Natto-natto, natto," sounded his loud childish voice up one street and down another, while we still lay snugly in bed. And at dusk there was the melancholy whistle of the blind masseur who tapped his way along in search of tired bodies to soothe into relaxation.

We went back to Tokyo on the most beautiful day of the whole summer. A typhoon had washed the atmosphere clean, the sky was a deep blue with enormous puffy clouds, and the mountains so clear that each tree stood out separately.

NHK's longest-running and one of its most popular programs, Nodo Jiman ("proud of my voice"), launched the national competition in 1948, an early version of the singing competition shows that now engulf the world.

Dancing to 1948's most popular song, Tokyo Boogie Woogie

Tokyo Boogie-Woogie/
Rhythm. Wowie Wowie/
My heart goes pit-a-pat. Tick-a-tack./
A song of the world. A happy song./
Tokyo Boogie-Woogie.

The first 'Miss Japan', Yamamoto Fujiko, 1950

Poster from the wildly popular movie Aoi Sammyaku *– 'Blue Mountain Range' – starring Hara Setsuko (second from right), the 'eternal virgin', in 1949*

203

. . . and a rather different one

From The China Lover *by Ian Buruma, 2008 – a fictionalized diary of a young occupation (1945 – 1952) officer, Donald Richie.*

Summer, when the cicadas rasp in the steaming heat, is my favorite season in Tokyo. It is then that the Japanese seem most natural, most themselves. In those early, less inhibited days after the war, strong workingmen emerged freshly scrubbed from the public baths, often in nothing but their white *furitoshi* neatly wrapped around their loins, leaving very little to the imagination. Tokyo, my Tokyo, the Tokyo of the common people, in August, was a banquet of honeyed curves and soft skin, displayed not to show off, but innocently, unself-consciously.

There were some establishments, near the blue lines, that catered to gentlemen of my persuasion, but they tended to be filled with young screamers of the kind that I loathed with a passion. Who needs a mincing little assistant hairdresser pawing the hair on your arms like some cheap harlot? I like men, not fake girls, or "sister boys," as the Japanese called them. Men were to be found lurking in the grounds of the Hanazono Shrine, a tradition that goes back at least three hundred years and, I'm happy to say, still persists. Truck drivers, construction workers, and the like went there to get quick relief from the old drag queens, who made up in technique for what they might have lost in looks. They were also much cheaper than the whores in the red lines. If they were drunk, or horny enough, the men would allow me to pleasure them for nothing.

But nothing delighted me more, before attending some important social function, than a little wallow in the Shinjuku mud. There I was, fresh from a hot encounter with a rough young hood behind Hanazono Shrine, bowing to the president of the Japanese Motion Pictures Association, or discussing the tea ceremony with the Dutch ambassador's wife.

Stand up pachinko parlor in 1949 – the most popular prize was tobacco.

Tobacco packs of the 1950s

The Emperors of Japan

Mutsuhito
the Meiji Emperor
1867 – 1912

Yoshihito
the Taisho Emperor
1912 – 1926

Hirohito
the Showa Emperor
1926 – 1989

Akihito
the Heisei Emperor
1989 - present

A Stewing Mass of People

Edward Seidensticker, widely recognized as one of the world's greatest translators of Japanese literature into English, writing in the 1960s

The roar about him is not just the roar of trains and taxicabs. It is also the roar of sinews and blood. A good Buddhist, in the days when the species survived, might have described Tokyo as smelling of meat; Walt Whitman might have said that it had the fine, clean smell of armpits. Tokyo is a stewing mass of people, and there are no beautiful, dead surfaces to distract one from the vitality once it is known.

Architect Charlotte Perriand described Tokyo at the time of her visit as a compress of ancient looking wooden buildings in the shadows of new colossi: "Tokyo 1956: modern buildings, small glass and cement fortresses, one after the other, housing the most unbelievable complexes: railway stations, metro, department stores, restaurants, theaters. At their feet a city of eight million inhabitants built from paper and wood."

Ishihara Yutaro, the 'Japanese James Dean', in 1956

Mishima Yukio buffs up in 1955, reflecting a nationwide fad for young men . . .

Mishima's Last Days

From Japanese Portraits: Pictures of Different People *by Donald Richie, 1987*

We often met during the summer before his death. All of Mishima's friends saw more of him during that 1970 summer. He phoned more, wrote more letters, paid more attention to us.

Movie street in Asakusa, 1957

. . . and leaving the courthouse in 1961 after losing a lawsuit over violation of privacy . . .

. . . and haranguing the euphemistically named Self Defense Forces at their Ichigaya HQ, dead center Tokyo, nine years later – moments after this, his head would part company with the rest of his body, courtesy his second, the kaishakunin, *who beheaded Mishima after the author had gutted himself.*

He was going away and would not see us again, but that we did not know then.

One late summer day he called again and asked me to join him at the Tokyo Hilton, a hotel he liked. Here he could, apparently unrecognized, book a room for writing or for other purposes.

He was not alone. With him was a young man whom I did not know but whose type I recognized. Limp, callow, probably literary — the kind of youth who resembled the young Mishima himself, the sort to whom the author now extended part of his patronage.

We sat in the mirrored bar and talked, and it became clear that the youth, a literary major (French), was a present for me. I was to continue, to take over, the patronage. Mishima told me this while the young man looked modestly down at his folded hands.

U.S. crazes make their way to Tokyo in the 1950s

Treasures

From City Life in Japan *by Ronald Dore, 1958*

With Japanese urban-population densities, moreover, the butcher and fishmonger is rarely more than five minutes' walk away and the savings of time and labour does not yet occupy a very high place in most housewives' scale of values. An ice-box, then, is a luxury. The sewing machine is primarily a means of economizing on clothing expenditure rather than a means of enjoyably occupying leisure. Some wives use it to supplement their income and for two or three widows in the ward it is their sole income source. An electric fan is another luxury, though one which is widely appreciated as a more effective substitute for the paper fans which are universally carried in the hot weather. The electric fan is the article most highly charged with prestige value, and the pride with which some housewives claimed to possess it was unmistakable.

The "three treasures" of the early 1950s: black and white television, refrigerator and electric washing machine

By the early 1960s, many more treasures were available

The Only Japanese Song to Reach #1 on the Billboard Charts

Ue wo Muite Aruko *(I Shall Walk Looking Up),* or Sukiyaki *as it became known in the West, was a 1963 smash hit for Sakamoto Kyu. The melody and music seemed upbeat to Western ears – ironically, the lyrics were penned by Ei Rokukuse after he left the massive Tokyo protest against the amendment of the Japan-U.S. security treaty in 1960 – Ei was depressed that despite the massive opposition, which disrupted U.S. President Eisenhower's visit to Japan, the opposition would fail. The Japanese lyrics refer to someone who looks up while they walk so that their tears won't hit the ground. Sukiyaki is a Japanese meat dish.*

Sakamoto died tragically in 1983 in the Japan Alps – one of the victims of the crash of JAL 123, which retains the record for deadliest single-aircraft accident in history.

From Billboard Magazine, *June 1963*

Louis Benjamin, the head of Britain's Pye Records, heard the song while visiting Japan on business in 1962, and brought it back for jazzman Kenny Bell to record. British DJs were not likely to be able to pronounce the real title, so Pye released the single under a Japanese name most people recognized: "Sukiyaki." As Newsweek pointed out, it was like releasing "Moon River" in Japan with the title "Beef Stew."

This movie's title is The Era of Irresponsibility

Hundreds of thousands mass in front of the Diet to protest the US-Japan security treaty and demand improved conditions for workers, June 1960.

Rollin', Rollin', Rollin'

Three-wheeled vehicles, relatively cheap to produce, provided much-needed budget transportation for people and goods. Daihatsu's Mizetto debuted in 1957.

Left: *The Honda Super Cub, launched in 1958, has become the top-selling wheeled vehicle in history.*
Right: *1958's Subaru 360*

Nissan's Bluebird 310, launched in 1959   Subway construction, early 1960s

From The House of Nomura *by Al Alletzhauser, 1990*
The pre-Olympic intercity trains still had wooden floors and each morning the smell of disinfectant in the cars, washed by hand the night before, was overpowering. Officials tried to cut down on the proliferations of bugs that burrowed into the wooden floorboards, but, according to Richard Devine, a scholar of Japanese history who moved to Tokyo in the late 1950s, the cleaners missed scrubbing behind the seat boards, the preferred breeding spot of fleas each September. 'You could always tell the people who were lucky enough to get a seat in the autumn since they were the ones who scratched all over.'

The Hibiya Line (left) begins operation between Kasumigaseki and Ebisu, March 1964, while the Tokyo Monorail (right), connecting the city's only airport of the day, Haneda, with Hamamatsucho Station in a non-stop run costing ¥250, began operations a month before the Olympics opened.

The first two bullet trains left Tokyo and Shin-Osaka Stations simultaneously, at 06:00 on 1 October 1964, ten days before the opening ceremony of the Tokyo Olympics.

More construction

Immersion

An excerpt from Donald Richie's diary, published in Tokyo, *1999*

10 March 1960. I go to my neighbourhood bath and stay a long time. I am very fond of it; it is the nearest thing to church, to the barber's, to a family.

They are all more or less alike, these baths, one to every neighbourhood, there must be thousands in Tokyo: a large barn-like building, tall chimney attached which begins smoking about two in the afternoon and continues to midnight. Inside, the building is divided into four equal-sized rooms. The back two (the baths) have a half-wall between; front two have a partition with a bath for the woman in charge so she can survey both sides (men's and women's) at the same time. The clothes are left in large baskets. Pay the money to the girl, sixteen yen; shampoo or a razor are five yen each; usually carry your own soap and towel.

Most of the bathers hold their towels in front of them when they go in; a habitual gesture; you see the same gesture in fully dressed men when they are cold; they cover their genitals. Originally I thought it was because of the girls working around but it is not. They pay no attention to the men nor the men to them. This is the country of the time and place for everything and the bath is not the place for sex.

Foreigners are told that they must wash outside the big tile baths, using the taps and little wooden buckets, and then get in. Well, maybe foreigners do but the Japanese certainly don't. On cold nights, like tonight, they climb in all dirty and let the communal water soak it off. At best the tap rinse is a mere token: feet, hands, maybe balls, but not often.

Everyone says the Japanese aren't dirty, that they are in fact clean. Well, I suppose they are cleaner than many, but no Japanese that I know bathes because he likes it. He bathes to get warm usually (once out and covered up, the body heat remains for the water is scalding) and he bathes to meet his friends. But not, I think, to get any cleaner than anyone else. Certainly not many bathe completely. Most men don't skin back and wash; and I have been told that women think it is immodest to get soap up inside. Once the bath is over, too, the dirty underwear goes right back on.

But it is nice in the bath and that is quite enough. You sit back and scald. It is relaxing. Perhaps that is why, in the bath and turning lobster-red, Japanese will say things they would otherwise not. Perhaps this is why one can always hear neighbourhood gossip in the bath.

One sits back in water which doesn't feel as dirty as it is only because it is so hot, looks at the picture (all bathhouses have one, a giant mural against the back wall, sometimes Western-type scenes, castle and sailboat and deer, sometimes a Chinese palace, not a Japanese castle in sight: all oil on tin and mildew), reads the advertisements (Love Beauty Salon, Suzuki's Expert TV Repair, Fame Barber Shop), and listens to the gossip.

Today I learn that that nice Mrs Watanabe down the street doesn't know that that nice Mr Watanabe—glasses and a wen—is keeping a girl young enough to be his daughter. Also learn that the eldest Hamada boy (much given to body building, has a bulging neck) is going to be the death of his parents, plays around with girls, and him so careful of his body too. Then someone says that if he had Mrs Watanabe around he'd keep two girls; another, that with parents like that he wonders the Hamada boy hadn't run away years ago.

Walking the Streets of Tokyo, 1960

From Belli Looks at Life and Law in Japan *by Melvin Belli, 1960*
To walk casually down the Ginza in Tokyo (if one can walk casually on a Japanese street) makes one conjecture whether Japan has laws regulating the driving of motor vehicles upon its thoroughfares. The little vehicles, operated by their just as diminutive Japanese drivers, dart in and out indiscriminately, apparently without following any rule, regulation or traffic pattern whatsoever.

From City Life in Japan *by Ronald Dore, 1958*
Girls skipping or playing hop-scotch, ball-bouncing to interminable songs with a younger brother or sister nodding drowsily on their backs. Boys wrestling, poring over comics, huddles into conspiratorial groups, playing games of snap with tremendous gusto and noise. There is generally, too, a group of their mothers passing the time of the day as they look benevolently on and prepare to mediate in quarrels. With their hair permanently waved or drawn into a bun at the back and clogs on their feet (nothing else could be slipped on and off so easily every time they enter and leave a house), a white long-

sleeved apron obscures the difference between those (younger ones) who wear skirt and blouse, and those (older ones) who wear *kimono*. One of them, perhaps, standing as she talks slightly bent forwards to balance the weight of a three-year-old tied astraddle here back, is on her way to the bath-house, a fact proclaimed by the metal bowl she carries in hands clasped under the baby's buttocks and by the washable rubber elephant with which he hammers abstractedly at the nape of her neck.

Promotional groups called chindonya *('chin' for the sound of the gong, 'don' for the sound of the drum, and 'ya' meaning 'business') were quite common in 1950s and 1960s Tokyo, where they advertised for pachinko parlors, other establishments and consumer brands. Rare today, they are viewed with nostalgia.*

As these crowds in Shinjuku and Ueno stations (top and above) circa 1960 attest, hiking, mountain-climbing and skiing became hugely popular, as Tokyoites' wealth increased enough for them to afford leisure time activities.

215

1964 – Tokyo Welcomes the Olympics

Japan's 350 Olympic athletes enter Tokyo's National Stadium on 10 October 1964. The torchbearer at the opening ceremony, Sakai Yoshinori, was born in Hiroshima — on 6 August 1945.

The closing ceremony

City Scenes, 1960s

Koenji Station, late 1960s

Arguably the most popular location for group photos in Tokyo, the Nijuubashi, 'Double Bridge', at the palace, circa 1970

What's Up with the 'L's and the 'R's?

A number of East Asian languages (Chinese, Japanese, Korean) don't have a distinction between the European-language 'l' and 'r' sounds. Consequently, Westerners may be entertained when East Asians pronounce 'fried rice' as 'flied lice'. The Japanese are similarly entertained when Westerners attempt to pronounce the double consonant sets, followed by a vowel, represented by the Roman letters 'ryu' and 'ryo', that occur regularly in Japanese. A mark of Japanese-language fluency is the degree to which one can pronounce these combinations.

Tokyo Station at its inception, circa 1914

Bibliography
Recommended books for further reading

- Adelstein, Joshua. *Tokyo Vice: An American Reporter on the Police Beat in Japan*. New York: Pantheon Books, 2009.
- Belli, Melvin. *Belli Looks at Life and Law in Japan*. Indianapolis: The Bobbs-Merrill Company, Inc., 1960.
- Bird, Isabella. *Unbeaten Tracks in Japan*. J. Murray, 1888.
- Bix, Herbert P. *Hirohito and the Making of Modern Japan*. New York: Harper-Collins, 2000.
- Buruma, Ian. *Behind the Mask*. New York: Penguin Group, 1984.
- Buruma, Ian. *The China Lover*. New York: The Penguin Press, 2008.
- Buruma, Ian. *Inventing Japan, 1853 – 1964*. New York: Modern Library, 2003.
- Buruma, Ian. *Year Zero*. New York: Penguin Press, 2013.
- Cook, Haruko Taya and Theodore F. *Japan at War – An Oral History*. New York: The New Press, 1992.
- Crow, Carl. *He Opened the Door to Japan*. New York and London: Harper & Brothers Publishers, 1939.
- Dower, John. *Embracing Defeat: Japan in the Aftermath of World War II*. New York: W.W. Norton & Company, 1999.
- Dower, John. *Ways of Forgetting, Ways of Remembering: Japan in the Modern World*. New York: New Press, 2012.
- Downer, Lesley. *Madame Sadayakko: The Geisha Who Bewitched the West*. New York: Gotham Books, 2003.
- Emmott, Bill. *Japanophobia*. New York: Times Books, 1993.
- Emmott, Bill. *The Sun Also Sets*. London: Simon and Schuster, 1989.
- Fallows, James. *More Like Us*. Boston: Houghton Mifflin Company, 1989.
- Fukuzawa, Yukichi. *The Autobiography of Yukichi Fukuzawa* (tr: Eiichi Kiyooka). New York: Columbia University Press, 1966.
- Futabatei Shimei. *Ukigumo* (tr.: Ryan, Marleigh Grayer). New York: Columbia University Press, 1965.
- Golden, Arthur. *Memoirs of a Geisha*. New York: Alfred A. Knopf, 1997.
- Gulick, Sidney. *Working Women of Japan*. New York: Missionary Education Movement of the United States and Canada, 1915.

- Johnston, William. *Geisha, Harlot, Strangler, Star*. New York: Columbia University Press, 2005.
- Keene, Donald ed. *Modern Japanese Literature: From 1868 to the Present Day*. Hong Kong: Tuttle Publishing, 1956.
- Kerr, Alex. *Dogs and Demons*. New York: Hill and Wang, 2001.
- Kokichi, Katsu. *Musui's Story – The Autobiography of a Tokugawa Samurai (tr. Craig, Teruko)*. First published 1843, translation: Tucson: The University of Arizona Press, 1988
- Kurosawa, Akira. *Something Like an Autobiography*. New York: Alfred A. Knopf, 1982.
- Kuwahara, Yasuo and Allred, Gordon, *Kamikaze*. New York: Ballantine Books, 1957.
- Longstreet, Stephen and Ethel. *Yoshiwara*. Tokyo: Tuttle Publishing, 1970.
- Maraini, Fosco. *Meeting with Japan*. New York: Viking Press, 1960.
- Maraini, Fosco and Sund, Harold. *Tokyo*. Amsterdam: Time-Life International, 1976.
- Manchester, William. *American Caesar: Douglas MacArthur, 1880 – 1964*. Boston: Little, Brown, 1978.
- Manchester, William. *Goodbye Darkness: A Memoir of the Pacific War*. Boston: Little, Brown, 1979.
- Mansfield, Stephen. *Tokyo: A Cultural History*. Oxford: Oxford University Press, 2009.
- Miller, Merle. *Plain Speaking: an Oral Biography of Harry S. Truman*. New York: Berkley Publishing Corp., 1974.
- Mitford, A.B. *Tales of Old Japan*. Boston: Tuttle Publishing, 1966 (originally published 1871).
- Morita, Akio. *Made in Japan*. New York: E.P. Dutton, 1986.
- Murakami, N., Murakawa, K., eds. *Letters Written by the English Residents in Japan: 1611 – 1623*. Tokyo: The Sankosha, 1900.
- Nakano, Yoshiko. *Where There Are Asians, There Are Rice Cookers*. Hong Kong: Hong Kong University Press, 2009.
- Norman, E. Hebert. *Japan's Emergence as a Modern State: Political and Economic Problems of the Meiji Period*. New York: Institute of Pacific Relations, 1940.
- Osugi, Sakae. *The Autobiography of Osugi Sakae* (tr: Marshall, Byron K.). Berkeley: University of California Press, 1992.
- Ozeki, Ruth. *A Tale for the Time Being*. New York: Viking, 2013.

- Peace, David. *Tokyo Year Zero*. New York: Alfred A. Knopf, 2007.
- Pilling, David. *Bending Adversity: Japan and the Art of Survival*. London: Allen Lane, 2013
- Ravina, Mark. *The Last Samurai: the Life and Battles of Saigo Takamori*. Hoboken: John Wiley & Sons, Inc. 2004.
- Richie, Donald. *The Films of Akira Kurosawa*. Berkeley: University of California Press, 1965.
- Richie, Donald. *Japanese Portraits: Pictures of Different People*. Tokyo: Tuttle Publishing, 1987.
- Richie, Donald. *Tokyo: A View of the City*. London: Reaktion Books Ltd., 1999.
- Schreiber, Mark. *The Dark Side: Infamous Japanese Crimes and Criminals*. Tokyo: Kodansha International, 2001.
- Schreiber, Mark. *Tokyo Confidential*. Tokyo: The East Publications, 2001.
- Seidensticker, Edward. *Low City, High City*. New York: Alfred A. Knopf, Inc., 1983.
- Smethurst, Richard J. *Takahashi Korekiyo, Japan's Keynes*. Cambridge (Massachusetts) and London: Harvard University Asia Center, 2007
- Smith, Patrick. *Japan: A Reinterpretation*. New York: Pantheon Books, 1997.
- Street, Julian. *Mysterious Japan*. Garden City: Doubleday, Page & Co., 1921.
- Vining, Elizabeth Gray. *Windows for the Crown Prince*. Philadelphia: J.B. Lippincott Co., 1952.
- Whiting, Robert. *Tokyo Underworld: The Fast Times and Hard Life of an American Gangster in Japan*. New York: Vintage Books, 1999.

Other English Works

- Agawa, Hiroyuki (tr.: Bester, John). *The Reluctant Admiral*. Tokyo: Kodansha International Ltd. 1979 (original Japanese title: Yamamoto Isoroku, 1969).
- Abbott, James Francis. *From Japanese Expansion and American Policies*. New York: The MacMillan Company, 1921.
- Alletzhauser, Al. *The House of Nomura*. London: Bloomsbury Publishing Ltd., 1990.
- Bamba, Tomoko. *The 'Office Ladies' Paradise: Inside and Out*. In The Japan Quarterly, Vol. 26, No. 2 (April-June 1979).
- Bacon, Alice. *A Japanese Interior*. Boston and New York: Houghton Mifflin and Co/Cambridge: The Riverside Press, 1894.
- Bacon, Alice. *Japanese Girls and Women*. Cambridge: The Riverside Press, 1899.

- Behr, Edward. *Hirohito: Behind the Myth*. New York: Villard Books, 1989.
- Benedict, Rose. *The Chrysanthemum and the Sword; Patterns of Japanese Culture*. Boston: Houghton Mifflin Company, 1946.
- Bickersteth, M. *Japan as We Saw It*. London: Sampson Low, Marston and Company, 1893.
- Birnbaum, Phyllis. *Modern Girls, Shining Stars, the Skies of Tokyo*. New York: Columbia University Press, 1999.
- Chamberlain, Basil Hall; Mason, W.B. *Travellers Guide to Japan*. London: Murray, 1907.
- *Changing Japan – Seen Through The Camera*. Tokyo: Asahi Shimbun Publishing Company, 1933.
- Cole, Robert. *Japanese Blue Collar: The Changing Tradition*. Berkeley: University of California Press, 1971.
- D'almeida, Anna. *A Lady's Visit to Manila and Japan*. London: Hurst and Blackett, 1863.
- Dekobra, Maurice. *My Japanese Holiday* (tr: Metcalfe Wood). New York: Greenberg, 1936.
- De Mente, Boye Lafayette. *The Japanese Have a Word for it*. Chicago: Passport Books, 1997.
- *Development of the Japanese Society since VJ Day*. Paper published by the Industrial College of the Armed Forces, No. L47-92. 12 March 1947.
- Faust, Allen K. *The New Japanese Womanhood*. New York: George H. Doran Co., 1926.
- Fujimoto, Taizo. *The Nightside of Japan*. London: Laurie, 1927.
- Gleason, George. *What Shall I Think of Japan?* New York: The MacMillan Company, 1921.
- Greey, Edward. *Young Americans in Japan*. Boston: Lee and Shepard Publishers, 1882.
- Grew, Joseph C. *Report from Tokyo*: A Message to the American People. New York: Simon and Schuster, 1942.
- Gunsaulus, Helen C. *The Japanese Sword and its Decoration*. Chicago: Field Museum of Natural History, 1924.
- Gunter, Archibald Clavering. *My Japanese Prince*. New York: The Home Publishing Company, 1904.
- Haskell, Helen Eggleston. *O-Heart-San*. Boston: L.C. Page and Company, 1908.
- Hearn, Lafcadio. *A Japanese Miscellany*. Tokyo: Charles E. Tuttle Co., 1954 (reprint of 1901 original).

- Hearn, Lafcadio. *Japan, An Attempt at Interpretation.* New York: The Macmillan Co., 1904.
- Ito, Hirobumi. *Commentary on the Constitution of the Empire of Japan.* 1906.
- Kimura, Ki. *Japanese Literature, Manners and Customs in the Meiji-Taisho Era.* Tokyo: Obunsha, 1957.
- Kipling, Joseph Rutyard. *From Sea to Sea: Letters of Travel and American Notes.* 1889.
- Kodama, Yoshio. *I Was Defeated.* Tokyo: Radiopress, 1959.
- Massing, Hede. *This Deception.* New York: Duell, Sloan and Pearce, 1951.
- Matsukata Reischauer, Haru. *Samurai and Silk.* Cambridge: The Belknap Press of Harvard University Press, 1986.
- Matsuoka, Yoko. *Daughter of the Pacific.* New York: Harper & Brothers, 1952.
- Mishima, Sumie Seo. *The Broader Way.* New York: The John Day Company, 1953.
- Morse, Edward S. *Japan Day By Day.* Boston and New York: Houghton and Mifflin, 1917.
- Murdoch, James, *The Tokugawa Epoch* (Volume III in A History of Japan). New York: Greenberg, 1926.
- Nakamoto, Hiroko. *My Japan 1930 – 1951.* New York: McGraw-Hill Book Company, 1970.
- Nippon Yusen Kaisha. *Handbook of Information for Shippers and Passengers.* Yokohama: Japan Mail S.S. Co., Ltd., 1904.
- Nitobe, Inazo. *Bushido: The Soul of Japan – An Exposition of Japanese Thought.* New York: G.P. Putnam & Sons, 1905.
- Nohara, Komakichi. *The True Face of Japan.* London: Jarrolds Publishers, 1936.
- Peace, David. *Occupied City.* London: Faber and Faber Ltd., 2009.
- Reischauer, Edwin O. *My Life Between Japan and America.* New York: Harper and Row, Publishers, 1986.
- Reischauer, Edwin O. *The Japanese.* Cambridge: The Belknap Press of Harvard University Press, 1977.
- Sakai, Saburo. *Samurai!* New York: E.P. Dutton and Co., Inc., 1957.
- Sansom, Sir George Bailey. *Japan: A Short Cultural History.* London: Cresset Press, 1931.
- Sansom, Katherine. *Living in Tokyo.* New York: Harcourt, Brace and Co., 1937.
- Sato, Hiroaki, *Legends of the Samurai.* New York: Overlook Press, 1995
- Satow, Ernest. *A Diplomat in Japan: The Inner History of the Critical Years in the Evolution of Japan When the Ports Were Opened and the Monarchy Restored.*

London: Seeley, Service & Co., 1921.

- Schom, Alan. *The Eagle and the Rising Sun.* New York: W.W. Norton & Co., 2004.
- Seagrave, Sterling and Peggy. *The Yamato Dynasty.* London: Bantam Press, 1999.
- Singer, Kurt (ed.: Storry, Richard). *Mirror, Sword and Jewel: A Study of Japanese Characteristics.* London: Croom Helm Ltd., 1973.
- Taylor, Bayard. *A Visit to India, China, and Japan in the Year 1853.* New York: G.P. Putnam, 1855.
- Terry, T. Philip. *Terry's Guide to the Japanese Empire.* Boston and New York, Houghton Mifflin, 1914.
- *The Edo-Tokyo Museum.* Tokyo: The Tokyo Metropolitan Foundation for History and Culture, 1998.
- Tomes, Robert. *The Americans in Japan: An Abridgment of the Government Narrative of the U. S. Expedition to Japan, under Commodore Perry.* Lanham: Rowman & Littlefield Publishers, Incorporated, 1873.
- Van Straelen, H. *The Japanese Woman Looking Forward.* Tokyo: Kyo Bun Kwan, 1940.
- Victoria, Brian Daizen. *Zen At War.* Lanham: Rowman & Littlefield Publishers, Inc., 2006.
- Vogel, Ezra F. *Japan's New Middle Class.* Berkeley: University of California Press, 1963.
- Wall Bingham, Marjorie; Hill Gross, Susan. *Women in Japan.* St. Louis Park: Glenhurst Publications, 1987.
- Wilde, Oscar. *The Decay of Lying – An Observation.* Essay published in *The Nineteenth Century*, London: C. Kegan Paul & Co, 1889.
- Young, John Russell. *Around the World with General Grant.* New York: Subscription Book Department, The American News Company, 1879.

Japanese-language works

- Humbert, Aime. *Bakumatsu Japan.* Tokyo: Toto Shobo, 1966 (Japanese translation of *Le Japon Illustré*, published in Paris in 1870).
- Ishii, Hiroshi, ed. *Memories of Shitamachi.* Tokyo: Taito Ward Arts and Culture Center, Shitamachi Museum, 2008.
- Kato, Hidetoshi, ed. *O-Edo Kaleidescope.* Tokyo: Agricultural and Fisheries Culture Society, 1991.
- Komeda, Sayoko, ed. *Women's Showa Era History.* Tokyo: Ootsuki Shoten, 1986.

- Takeuchi, Makoto, ed. *400 years of Nihonbashi and Ginza*. Tokyo: Miyaobi Publishing, 2013.
- Tamai, Tetsuo, ed. *Resurrecting Tokyo in the Meiji Era*. Tokyo: Kakegawa Arts and Sciences Publishing, 1992.
- *History of Tokyo Station*. Tokyo: JTB, 2000.
- *High School Japanese History*. Tokyo: Jikkyo Shuppan, 2008.
- *Meiji Historical Data Book*. Tokyo: Meiji Tosho Shuppan, 2006.
- *Meiji-Taisho 60-year History in Pictures*. Tokyo: Mainichi Shinbunsha, 1956.
- *History*. Tokyo: Kyoiku Shuppan, 2007.
- *Showa Times* (a 64-issue pictorial history of the Showa era). Tokyo: DeAgostini Japan, 2007 – 2008.
- *Taisho and Showa Lifestyle Memorial Collection*. Tokyo: Koshu Shobo Shinsha, 2001.

Image Credits

- Cover page, 183: F. Maraini, *Meeting with Japan*, 1960
- Page 16 (street scene): E. Reischauer, *The Japanese*, 1977
- Pages 17 (city at dusk), 29 (stone statue), 53 (Ginza at night), 208, 211 (*chindonya*), 214 (Koenji Station), 215: H. Sund, *Tokyo*, 1977
- Pages 20 (all), 61 (Tsukiji), 77 (top), 92, 105: Tamai, T., ed., *Resurrecting Tokyo in the Meiji Era*, 1992
- Page 71 (three people): L. Downer, *Madame Sadayakko*, 2003
- Pages 123 (people), 163: Ishii, H., ed., *Memories of Shitamachi*, 2008 (Japanese)
- Pages 131, 160: Komeda, S., ed., *Women's Showa Era History*, 1986 (Japanese)
- Page 181 (all): Morita, A., *Made in Japan*, 1986

Additional images sourced from (all Japanese works)

- Kato, H., ed., *O-Edo Kaleidescope*, 1991
- *History of Tokyo Station*, 2000
- *High School Japanese History*, 2008
- *Meiji Historical Data Book*, 2006
- *Showa Times*, 2007 – 2008

Acknowledgments

Usual comment here—all errata are my own, all enhancements due to my many advisors. I gratefully offer pride of place here to Mark Schreiber, a four-decade resident of Tokyo and a leading authority on the history of the city. Mark generously read the manuscript closely and suggested a number of solid improvements, saving me from a score of indelicacies, miscues and outright howlers. *Tales of Old Tokyo* is substantially better because of his learned input. Other valued advisors include (in alphabetical order) Masahiko Agata, Deven Arora, Gordon Berger, Sloan K. Carr, Cory Christensen, Matthew Crabbe, Chris Dillon, Angie Eagan, Graham Earnshaw, Paul French, Ian Gow, Terry Graham, Eric Hess, Keith (Katsuyoshi) Hori (thanks for both *shochu* and library), Tetsuo Hossho, Johann Huber, Jack Jackson, Chris Japp, Fumio Kanda, Chiharu Lopez, Jeff Loucks (thanks for fine *shitamachi* lodgings), Akiko Miwata, Patrick Moreton, Aki Murakami (thanks for all the Japanese-language material and the Kansai perspective), Brian Nelson, Peter Nunn, Dan O'Brien, Patricia O'Keefe, Takahiko Raijo, Dave Shapiro (more library and fine *shitamachi* lodgings), Christina Shmigel, Houston Spencer, Hatsue Takahashi, Tom Watanabe and Scott Williams. Honorable mention to Jerry Hegerty, who founded (in 1970) and ran until his death in 2001 the Rising Sun in the Yotsuya district of Tokyo, the first British-owned pub in the post-war city and a watering hole for a number of the above.

In addition to a wealth of original sources from the mid 19th to the mid 20th centuries, I've been fortunate to have some more recent, outstanding works on the history and culture of the city and country to refer to and quote from, including Jake Adelstein's *Tokyo Vice*; Herbert Bix's *Hirohito and the Making of Modern Japan*; Ian Buruma's *Behind the Mask*, *The China Lover*, *Inventing Japan* and *The Wages of Guilt*; Haruko and Theodore Cook's *Japan at War*; John Dower's *Embracing Defeat* and *Ways of Forgetting, Ways of Remembering*; Leslie Downer's *Madame Sadayakko*; Bill Emmott's *Japanophobia* and *The Sun Also Sets*; James Fallows' *More Like Us*; Donald Keene's *Modern Japanese Literature*; Alex Kerr's *Dogs and Demons*; Akira Kurosawa's *Something Like an Autobiography*; Stephen and Ethel Longstreet's *Yoshiwara*; Stephen Mansfield's *Tokyo: a Cultural History*; Akio Morita's *Made in Japan*; Ruth Ozeki's *A Tale for the Time Being*; David Peace's *Tokyo Year Zero* and *The Occupied City*; Haru Matsukata Reischauer's *Samurai and Silk*; Donald Richie's *Japanese Portraits* and *The Films of Akira Kurosawa* and *Tokyo* (among other writings); Mark Schreiber's *The Dark Side* and *Tokyo Confidential*; Patrick Smith's *Japan: A Reinterpretation*; and

Robert Whiting's *Tokyo Underworld*. Details in the bibliography.

Thanks also to my colleagues, some of the best people I've ever worked with, for their tolerance of my hobby: Doris Cao, Chen Baizhu, Eli Chen, Dai Fang, Sunny Donenfeld, Shantanu Dutta, Jim Ellis, Brigitte Engel, Suh-Pyng Ku, Lisa Li, Tracy Lin, Paul Luo, Lv Wei, Samantha Meng, Greg Patton, Bernice Taylor, Phil Wang, Sophia Wang, Winnie Wang, Cindy Wu, Emma Xi, Fernando Zapatero, Jane Zhao, Zhou Lin and the rest of our colleagues at USC Marshall and the Antai College in Shanghai.

Finally, thanks to Ms. Bo for tolerating my endless whinging during the carpentry, and to my mother Charlotte for her decades-long forbearance.

With the support of the above-mentioned people and sources, plus that of Earnshaw Books, I trust I've been able to construct a work with lasting value, to properly honor the city I visit often, and miss daily.

John Darwin Van Fleet, Shanghai, Spring Festival, 2015